Jenny,

I thought you might need one of these for your 1st apartment. I know you're not in Girl Scouts now but you use to and went to Camp Chance so hope you enjoy this book.

Love,
Aunt Sandy

Hope's Bounty

Recipes and Remembrances

From Girl Scouts of Riverland Council in Southwestern Wisconsin, Northeastern Iowa, and Southeastern Minnesota

Girl Scouts
Where Girls Grow Strong

Hope's Bounty
*Recipes and Remembrances
From Girl Scouts of Riverland Council
in Southwestern Wisconsin,
Northeastern Iowa, and Southeastern Minnesota*

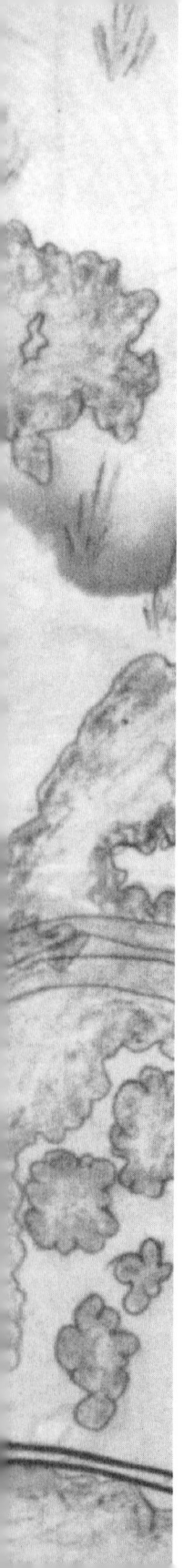

Published by Girl Scouts of Riverland Council, Inc.

Copyright © 2002 by
Girl Scouts of Riverland Council, Inc.
2710 Quarry Road
La Crosse, Wisconsin 54654
1-800-78-SCOUT
email: girlscouts@centuryinter.net
www.gsriverland.com

This cookbook is a collection of favorite recipes,
which are not necessarily original recipes.

All rights reserved. No part of this publication may be reproduced
in any form or by any means, electronic or mechanical, including photocopy
and information storage and retrieval systems, without permission
in writing from the publisher.

Library of Congress Catalog Number: 2001 131752
ISBN: 0-9711920-0-6

Edited, Designed, and Manufactured by
Favorite Recipes® Press
An imprint of

FRP

P. O. Box 305142
Nashville, Tennessee 37230
800-358-0560

Art Director: Steve Newman
Book Design: Jim Scott
Project Manager: Linda A. Jones

Manufactured in the United States of America
First Printing: 2002
5,000 copies

The Girl Scout Promise:

On my honor, I will try:

To serve God and my country,

To help people at all times,

And to live by the Girl Scout Law.

The Girl Scout Law:

I will do my best to be

honest and fair, friendly and helpful,

considerate and caring, courageous and strong, and

responsible for what I say and do.

And to respect myself and others, respect authority,

use resources wisely, make the world a better place,

and be a sister to every Girl Scout.

In Commemoration of Hope Lodge

A Year-Round Dining and Program Center At Camp Ehawee, Mindoro, Wisconsin

Built 2001

We would like to thank the following individuals who helped make this cookbook a reality and thus helped make Hope Lodge a reality:

Camille Smith,
Development Chair,
Seneca, Wisconsin

Robert Smith,
Marketing Co-Chair,
La Crosse, Wisconsin

Linda Benjamin,
Marketing Co-Chair,
Holmen, Wisconsin

Rick Brown,
La Crosse, Wisconsin

Donna Loveland,
Onalaska, Wisconsin

Janet Roth,
La Crosse, Wisconsin

Gina Wilkins,
Onalaska, Wisconsin

Mary Rohrer,
Executive Director

Sally K. Snow,
Assistant Executive Director for Fund Development

Capital Campaign

We would like to thank the following individuals for their hard work and dedication to the Capital Campaign to build the Hope Lodge, which allowed the Girl Scouts of Riverland Council to

"Make a Promise...For All the Girls"!

Honorary Chairs

Gail K. Cleary
Kristine Cleary
Sandra Cleary
The Cleary Management Corporation
Cleary-Kumm Foundation

Campaign Cabinet

Patricia M. Heim, J.D.,
   Chair,
   Attorney,
   Parke O'Flaherty, LTD
Dirk L. Gasterland,
   Vice Chair
   President, The Coulee State Bank
Linda Benjamin
   Optometric Technician
   Franciscan Skemp Healthcare
Tom Farrell
   President,
   People's State Bank
   Prairie du Chien

Michael J. Flanagan
   Flanagan Financial, Inc.
Jean Gitz Bassett
   Radio Broadcasting (Retired)
   Community Advocate
Grace Hanson
   Community Advocate
Betty Heuslein
   Community Advocate
Palmer "Duffy" Hoffland
   President, Fortress Bank, Viroqua
Geoffrey Klos
   Vice President,
   Robert W. Baird
Meredyth Lillejord
   Owner
   Lillejord and Sandmire Interior Design
Donna Loveland, R.D.
   Nutrition Consultant
Nancy Mannstedt
   Owner, Allure Salon
Lorna Schini
   Community Advocate

Joanne Selkurt, M.D.
   Pediatrician,
   Gundersen Lutheran
Thomas Sleik, J.D.
   Hale Skemp Hanson Skemp and Sleik
Eleanor St. John
   KQEG Television
David Trapp
   David Trapp Agency
Mary Jo Werner, CPA
   Partner,
   Wipfli Ullrich Bertelson

Building Chairman

Jack Jansky, La Crosse
   (WWTC—retired)

Council President

Donald Smith

Executive Director

Mary Rohrer

Girl Scouts Facts

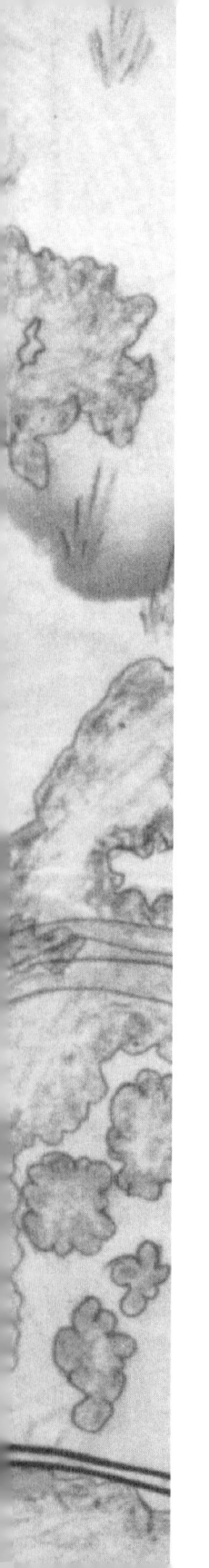

Founding Data—
Juliette Gordon Low, founder, organized the first group of girls on March 12, 1912, in Savannah, Georgia.

- Incorporated in Washington, D.C., June 10, 1915.
- Relocated to New York City.
- Chartered by the United States Congress, March 16, 1950.
- Girl Scouts of Riverland Council incorporated, 1917.

90 years old—
Girl Scouts is a value based program that gives girls from all socio-economic levels a chance to develop their potential, to make friends, and to become a vital part of their community. Based on ethical values, Girl Scouting opens up a wide world of opportunity for girls, role modeled by successful female adult mentors. The Girl Scouts' unique and sole focus is to meet the special needs of girls in an all-girl environment.

Its Program—
Is a continuous adventure in learning offering every girl a broad range of activities in 200 merit badges—activities which address both her current interests and her future role as a woman. Activities encouraging self-learning introduce girls to the excitement in the worlds of science, the arts, the out-of-doors, and people. Girls grow strong in skill and in self-confidence. They have fun, they make new friends, and through meaningful community service, they acquire a unique understanding about themselves and others.

Girl Scouts of the U.S.A.—
The largest organization for girls in the world. It is open to all girls ages five through seventeen (or kindergarten through grade twelve) who subscribe to its ideals as stated in the Girl Scout Promise Law. One out of every six girls in our council is a Girl Scout. One out of every nine girls in the U.S.A. is a

Girl Scout. It is a part of a worldwide family of girls and adults in 136 free-world countries through its membership in the World Association of Girl Guides and Girl Scouts (WAGGGS).

Its Members

There are approximately 3.4 million adult and girl members in the Girl Scouts of the USA. Girl Scouts of Riverland Council serves approximately 5,000 girls and adult volunteers annually. Only 1 percent of the adult workforce is paid.

2,583,500 girls nationwide in five program levels:

- Daisy (Kindergarten)
- Brownies (First through Third Grade)
- Juniors (Third through Sixth Grade)
- Cadettes (Sixth through Ninth Grade)
- Seniors (Ninth through Twelfth Grade)

Girls and leaders participate in Girl Scouting through group activities in troops and groups including U.S.A. Girl Scouts Overseas in more than 80 countries. Members of overseas troops come from U.S. military and civilian families living abroad. There are 525 Girl Scout troops in Riverland Council.

Its Structure

Girl Scout troops are organized by Girl Scout councils—313 in the U.S.A. Riverland Council is a local unit chartered by the national organization to administer and develop Girl Scouting in ten countries in three states with seventy-five communities. Riverland Council is headquartered in La Crosse, Wisconsin. For more information, visit our website at www.gsriverland.com.

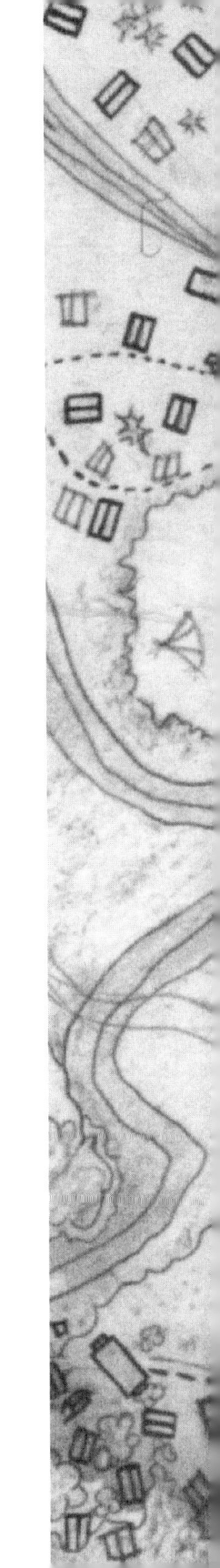

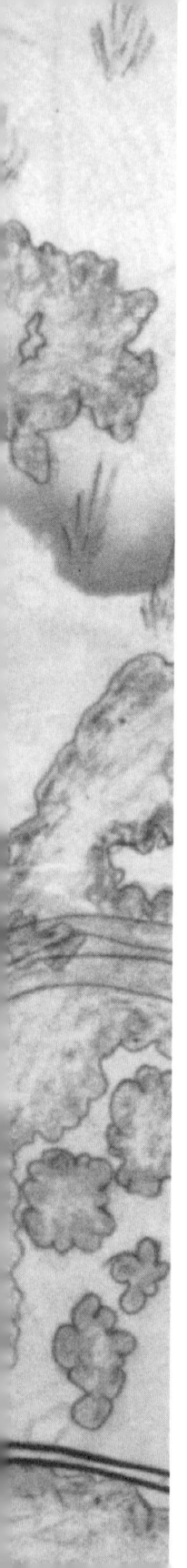

Table of Contents

Foreword
10

Preface
12

History of Girl Scouts of the U.S.A.
—Riverland Council
14

Celebrating at Camp Ehawee: Fifty Years Young
22

Outdoor Cooking
(Recipes for the Grill or Campfire)
24

Healthy Nibbles
(Appetizers and Snacks)
50

Girl Scout Greens
(Salads and Side Dishes)
68

Regional Fare
(Recipes from the Upper Mississippi Valley)
86

Rush Hour Cooking
(Recipes in Thirty Minutes or Less)
108

Girl Scout Desserts
(And Other Sweet Things)
126

Contributors
154

Index
156

Order Information
160

Foreword

Born and raised in La Crosse, Wisconsin, my mother, father, and I shared a love of learning and discovery. This led to my participation in Girl Scouting, because my mother, L. Hope Kumm, knew that Girl Scouting was a perfect match for me. Mother served as my first troop leader and I, in turn, served as the first troop leader for my two daughters, Sandra and Kristine. Our lives were mingled with the richness of the southwestern Wisconsin region and Girl Scouts.

Father was not pleased when he learned that my first experience in traveling away from home actually involved a rental of the Boy Scout camp. Thus, Mother and Father went on an expedition with the help of many other volunteers, chaired by Marie Schanzle at that time, and in 1951 they found the perfect property for Camp Ehawee, a 305-acre site along the backwaters of the Black River near Melrose-Mindoro, Wisconsin. "Ehawee" is Ho Chunk for "laughing maidens," interpreted as young women and girls experiencing fun and camaraderie together. A Girl Scout contest among girl members of the council designated this very appropriate name for our resident camp.

L. Hope Kumm

As a Girl Scout leader, Mother taught us that values are a time-honored tradition of family and community. She knew our roots were embedded in our hometown spirit and that through Girl Scouting you educate the whole person: healthy in body, and strong in mind and spirit.

Mother represents the first generation of our four-generation Girl Scout family. Following in Hope's footsteps, my daughter, Kristine, is leading a Daisy Girl Scout troop Fall 2001 for her daughters, Megan and Sara. My daughter Sandra tells me that her three-year-old daughter, Katherine, will surely be a Girl Scout. Girl Scouting has demonstrated through the years how it is a perfect match for all families. I cannot think of any one special activity over time that has been so popular with girls of all ages and backgrounds as Girl Scouting. I know of no other place where adventure, learning, friendship, and fun all converge in such a wonderfully supportive and safe environment.

This cookbook honors the contributions of the Upper Mississippi River Valley and reflects the ever-changing make-up of the seventy-five communities that are part of the Girl Scouts of Riverland Council. Mother became the council board president and I did likewise. Currently, I am a member of the National Board of Girl Scouts of the U.S.A. When coming home from meetings at National Headquarters, New York City, it always reinforces in my mind the wonderful contributions that women make to mentor our young girls and teenagers today. It also makes me feel how fortunate I am to come home to southwestern Wisconsin, rich in culture and traditions, and filled with hardworking, church-going people who value home and family. How could Girl Scouts have better partners?

We are so honored that this lodge at Camp Ehawee is a legacy to my mother, L. Hope Kumm, my children's grandmother, and great-grandmother of Sara, Megan, Katherine, William Russell, and Russell Philip. We think of Hope Lodge as living in the hearts of many generations. We know that nothing loved is ever lost and my mother was loved so much!

I am honored to write the dedication of this cookbook to my Mother in celebration of fifty years of Camp Ehawee and its newest edition, Hope Lodge, a first-ever year-round program and dining center. Our family hopes that this new facility will be a centerpiece and gathering place for nurturing positive values for all girls who arrive at this very special place, Camp Ehawee!

Gail K. (Kumm) Cleary

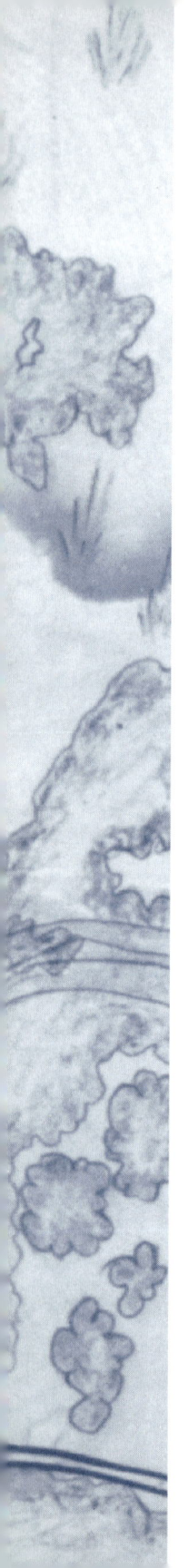

Preface

When discussing this special celebration project for ninety years of Girl Scouting and fifty years of Girl Scout Camp Ehawee, our committee not only wanted to create wonderful recipes but also desired to honor the contributions that the Mississippi River Valley folks make in this wonderful part of our land.

Southwestern Wisconsin, northeast Iowa, and southeastern Minnesota are filled with small rural communities, over seventy-five of them, and woven into their special fabric are positive contributions each and every person has made. Our celebration settled on a historical adventure, chronicled as a gathering of food, culture, history, and tradition! The reason? Because the common threads that unite us are one and the same—family, faith, and home. The traditions of our communities are evidenced through the recipes, the design of this cookbook, the historical features, and everything you have ever wanted to commemorate. What a magnanimous way to celebrate Girl Scouting!

People are drawn to our area because of the sense of knowing that this is truly home. This is illustrated through the recipes, the gourmet cooks, the Midwestern cooks, the family cooks, the chefs, and all the historians who want to be part of a sense of belonging to the Coulee Region. You will find a delightful assortment of recipes and historical information that reflects the lifestyles of our contributors. Our artwork, chapter openers, and the additional sidebars were chosen to display our vibrant people and communities, all of whom are woven into and are a part of Girl Scouting.

One out of every six girls in this council joins Girl Scouting! What a significant impact to the lives of children and their families. Riverland Council serves girls in ten counties of southwestern Wisconsin, northeast Iowa, and southeastern Minnesota. A recent study showed that 81 percent of girls identified summer camp as their most rewarding Girl Scout program activity. We believe camp offers the best in Girl Scouting because it provides opportunities for girls to make new friends and at the same time learn new leadership skills. We believe it is the perfect outdoor classroom where girls swim, ride horseback, and cross-country ski, all the time learning about their environment and their responsibility to protect it. For many girls, it is not only the first time away from home but also the first opportunity to make independent decisions that develop new self-confidence and self-sufficiency. This unique all-girl setting allows them to test their limits without the pressure of any competition or risk of failure.

Through your support to this unique historical cookbook, you will help us expand our program activities and strengthen our programs for all girls and teenage women. We want to ensure that no girl is left out of Girl Scouting.

Volunteers worked to choose special features that help illustrate who we are in the upper Midwest. We hope that these contributions will inspire readers to treat each recipe as an artistic creation, and each tradition and historical feature as a special treasure, just as we and future generations, will treasure our newest *pièce de résistance*, Hope Lodge: our year-round dining and program center at our beloved Camp Ehawee!

Thanks to these treasures, Girl Scouts truly is where girls grow healthy in body and strong in spirit!

Mary Rohrer, Executive Director

History of Girl Scouts of the U.S.A.—Riverland Council

Although they were pioneers in Girl Scouting in La Crosse, Wisconsin, and Mrs. M. B. Skundberg and C. I. Anderson started their troop in 1926, it was really Mrs. J. E. McConnell who, in 1917, founded Girl Scouting. A Girl Scout community was initially formed with this first troop, Troop #1.

Miss Bertha Shuman organized Troop #2, and it was Miss Shuman's continuing enthusiasm and hard work that kept Girl Scouting growing during the trying years of the '20s and '30s. Her clippings and scrapbook collection became the beginnings of an archive, giving us the history of Girl Scouts of Riverland Council.

Because of Miss Shuman's love of the out-of-doors, she brought the experience of camping to the Girl Scouts at the very beginning. She directed camp for the early troops during 1923 to 1927 at Spring Banks near Sparta, Wisconsin. Camp programs were much the same, as the purpose of camping has always been fun in the out-of-doors.

Girl Scouts in the 1940s learn teamwork from building a campfire.

Because Girl Scout camping became so popular—and because it was the only way the girls in those days were given permission to try out camping—Miss Shuman rented Boy Scout Camp Decorah in the late '20s. By the mid '30s, she also rented YMCA's Camp Bradford to meet the popularity of the Girls Scouts. Soon troops were forming from Holmen, Viroqua, Hillsboro, West Salem, Galesville, Sparta, and Tomah so each community of girls could enroll in Miss Shuman's camping programs.

These troops were called "lone troops" because volunteer leaders had no help—studying handbooks on their own and doing their best in leading girls in troops as large as sixty in number. Girl Scouting quickly became a leadership challenge!

Becoming an officially chartered council and electing its first volunteer president, Mrs. R. C. Whelpley, in 1931, the council had assigned to it the first professional worker by the National Organization for the 250 girls enrolled as Girl Scout members. After a short tenure, Mrs. Gen (Bert) Welthe succeeded the first employee, staying on as the executive director for thirty-four years. In 1977, Mrs. Frances (Robert) Skemp was elected council president, appointing Mary Rohrer as the successor to Gen Welthe upon Mrs. Welthe's retirement.

During the World War II years, Girl Scouting became the number one popular activity, with community service and badge-earning activities the cornerstone to the program. Girl Scouts collected nylon and silk stockings for the manufacture of powder bags. They saved used bed linens for wound dressings, and began baking cookies for the American Red Cross and the U.S.O.

In the 1940s, Girl Scouts recycled tin, rubber, and waste fats.

Girl Scouts opened up a new program in 1956 called "Brownies" for girls ages six through eight, and offered "day camping" for this age group, growing to eleven day camping programs today. Unique to "day camping," from its beginnings to the present, is that it has always been 100 percent volunteer-directed. Currently over 1,000 girls in ten counties in three states participate in this community-sponsored program.

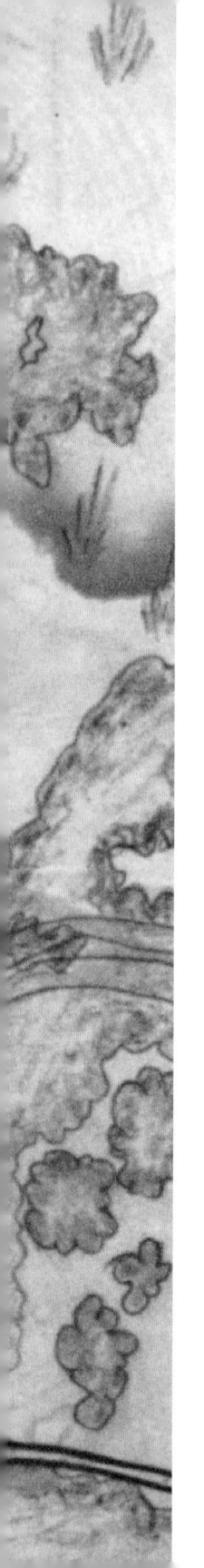

The first official Girl Scout cookie sale began in 1931, when the idea caught on in the Midwest but the sale had its roots in 1917 Philadelphia. Asked by the Philadelphia Gas Company that year to demonstrate baking cookies in their new gas oven in the store window, the Girl Scout troops of Philadelphia unknowingly staged the first-ever Girl Scout cookie sale.

In 1931, Mrs. Albert Funk and Mrs. R. G. McDonald of La Crosse considered this a grand idea, and organized the baking of 4,834 dozen sugar cookies through the local Erickson Bakery, selling them at twenty cents per dozen. From this modest beginning came great things: In 2001, the Girl Scouts of Riverland Council took orders for over 317,000 boxes of cookies!

It's annual cookie sale time for both Girl Scouts and their younger Brownie Scout sisters. Members of troops throughout the city are taking house-to-house orders in their annual campaign to raise funds in this longtime celebrated annual event.

According to Dirk Gasterland, president, Coulee State Bank and first vice president of the Girl Scout Board, this amounts to seven cookies per every man, woman, and child in the council's jurisdiction. During the cookie-selling season, Girl Scouts outsell Keebler and Nabisco cookies!

Camp Ehawee, the Girl Scouts' own camp property, was founded and developed as the camp that cookies built. Marie Schwanzle led the search for a camp of its own just for the girls. Local service clubs assisted with the site acquisition at the encouragement of Roy and Hope Kumm. Dissatisfied because their daughter Gail and her troop, along with Gail's mother Hope, as the volunteer leader, had to rent Boy Scout Camp Decorah when the Boy Scouts were finished camping, Roy and Hope joined the Marie Schwanzle search for a Girl Scout camp property, and thus Camp Ehawee was born in

Winning name of the new Girl Scout camp near Mindoro, Wisconsin, was entered by Jacqueline Kramer, shown receiving her award of $5 in Girl Scout equipment from Mrs. Phil A. Schwanzle, chairman on the campsite development committee.

Mrs. John Kramer, La Crosse, Jacqueline's mother, is the Troop 27 leader, and received a prize for the troop identical to that for the winning name.

Jacqueline wrote this letter to explain her choice: "I chose the name Camp Ehawee because it means Camp of the Laughing Maidens. Bringing a group of girls together for a single purpose—to grow in friendships, to be joyful, to learn to obey orders to become skillful in many things—this should make for much joy and laughter."

1951. Named in a Girl Scout contest among its members, Girl Scout Jacqueline Kramer's entry won out with her name "Ehawee," interpreted in Ho Chunk as "laughing maidens."

Today Camp Ehawee is a 305-acre site complete with two winterized year-round lodges—Berthe Shuman and Nakomis Lodges, sleeping fifty girls in each lodge. Camp Ehawee also includes a swimming pool; the Sandy Gordon Ballpark; an outdoor amphitheatre; three sleeping units—Sacajewea, Minnehaha, and Marinuka—with platform tents, flush toilets and running water, and activity houses; and the camp director's home. In 2001, the newest addition to Camp Ehawee was Hope Lodge, a year-round dining and program center including a trading post, state-of-the-art kitchen, performing arts, first aid station, bathrooms, check in/check out, and camp director's administrative offices. The AFL-CIO and its labor unions have always from the beginning been a part of the building projects at Camp Ehawee, with donated labor and materials.

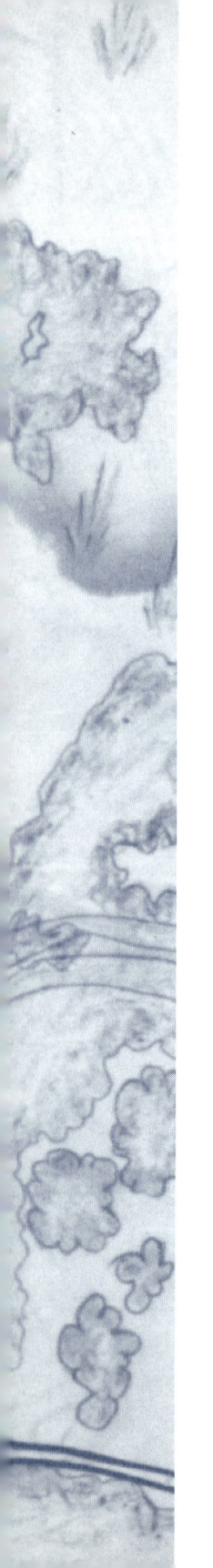

Today, more than 1,200 girls attend the resident camp summer season, with an employee staff of forty-five; and over 6,500 girls and adult volunteers enjoy Camp Ehawee year-round.

The council's in-town La Crosse–headquartered service center was housed in a second-story rental walkup until 1980 when a first-ever capital campaign raised $350,000 to construct its own service center adjacent to the Boy Scout Gateway Council service center in Hixon Forest.

A recipient of the State of Wisconsin first place Architectural Award for its passive solar design, the winning design was submitted by Hackner, Schroeder, Roslansky (HSR). A capital campaign co-chaired by Matt Heimerman, retired president of the Coulee State Bank of La Crosse, Wisconsin, and Gail K. Cleary, president, Cleary Management Corporation, raised 100 percent of the funds. Don Smith, senior vice president, La Crosse Lutheran Hospital, chaired the building committee.

Standing at the entrance to their tent in Unit No. 1, two girls receive handbooks and other reading materials from Shirley Julian of Maiden Rock, an assistant leader at the camp. Scouts are Jill Horswill and Judith Tooke. (Camp Ehawee 1950s)

Ten years later, a second capital campaign entitled "Campaign for Character" launched the first-ever combined Girl Scout and Boy Scout capital campaign for maintenance and capital improvement projects at Camp Ehawee and Camp Decorah, raising more than $1.2 million the first time for both camps, evenly divided between the two organizations. Nationally, this was the first ever funding collaboration between the Girls Scouts and Boy Scouts.

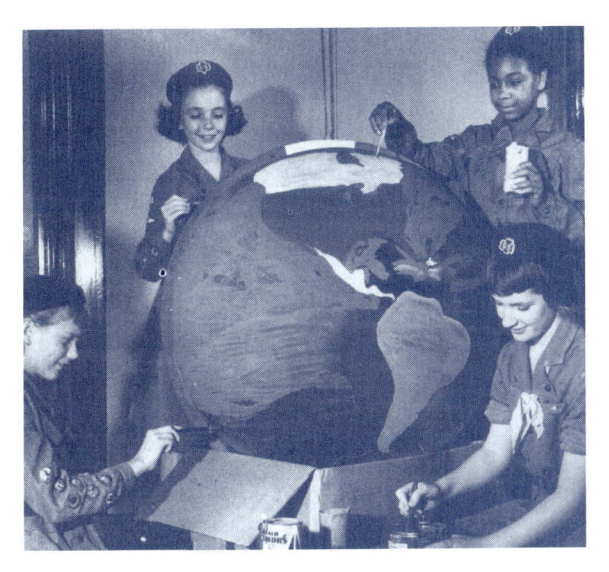

Girl Scouts explored world friendship in the 1950s.

As a result of this successful endeavor, the local chapter of the Association of Fundraising Professionals recognized campaign leaders Thomas Sleik, Dr. Ruth Dalton, Dirk Gasterland, and Gail Cleary for their outstanding achievement.

"To Make A Promise... For All The Girls" was developed in 2001 to build a year-round program and dining center at Camp Ehawee, Hope Lodge, in honor of Hope Kumm. After much analysis with the construction company TCI, volunteer building chair, Jack Jansky, and council president, Don Smith, determined it would be more economical to build a new year-round dining lodge, rather than expanding the existing seasonal facility. When eliciting reaction from leaders and parents, the response was unanimous: "It's about time!"

In Unit No. 1, the girls at left are preparing for a meal while Diane Armstrong brings in an armload of wood. At the fireplace, from left, are: Elsa Larson, Gretchen Hetherington, and Pat Anderson. (Camp Ehawee 1950s)

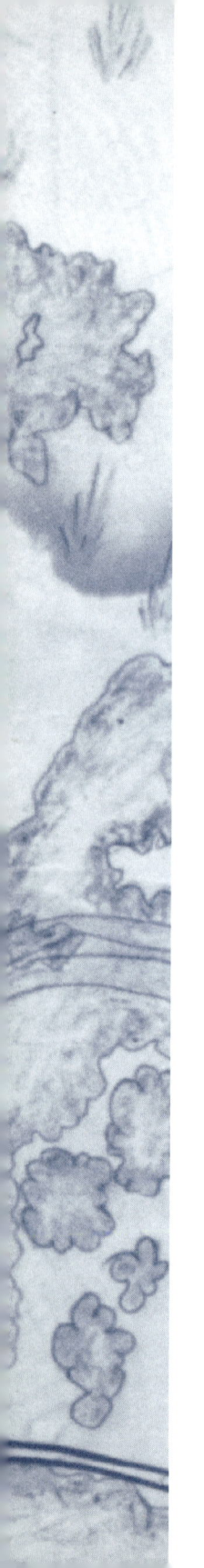

The new facility, Hope Lodge is the *pièce de résistance* for Camp Ehawee, fulfilling the dream of Girl Scouting for every girl everywhere. Hope Lodge has a capacity that is twice that of its predecessor, accommodating 275 for dining and 400 for activities. No longer will girls be turned away for lack of space. This new facility puts girls at the center of Camp Ehawee, giving them equal opportunity to learn and assume leadership in a supportive all-girl environment.

This new facility gives girls the opportunity to learn, take risks, and assume leadership roles. Through Camp Ehawee, Girl Scouts have the power to change lives, reaching out to more girls than ever before.

A 1950s master plan for Camp Ehawee, new Girl Scout recreation and camping center in northern La Crosse County, is being prepared for future development programs. A survey of the camp was made to secure data for the master plan. Mrs. Marie (Mrs. Phil) Schwanzle, camp development committee chairman, is shown explaining a camp map.

With Mrs. Schwanzle, from left, are: Julian H. Salomon, New York, national Girl Scout staff camp consultant; C. A. Hammond Jr., Madison, landscape architect of the bureau of engineering, Wisconsin State Planning Board; Clyde Bourett and Orville Hays of the water development committee.

The "To Make A Promise...For All The Girls" campaign, chaired by attorney Pat Heim and Vice Chair Dirk Gasterland, continues to need capital and endowment support. Serving over 5,000 girls and adults in more than 500 troops in seventy-five rural and urban communities, Girl Scouts welcomes your financial support to a program that today is ninety years strong! You can help impact tomorrow's girls with your financial gift to one of the oldest youth programs in southwestern Wisconsin, southeastern Minnesota, and northeast Iowa, the Girl Scouts of Riverland Council. Your gift will permanently endow our Camp Ehawee for many future generations of girls!

Three generations active in Girl Scouting in La Crosse in the 1960s. Mrs. Phil Schwanzle, chairman of camping in the council, began her Scouting as a leader of her daughter Sally's Girl Scout troop at Campus School in 1938 and has been active since that time.

In the 1960s, Mrs. G. William (Sally) Cremer, along with Mrs. Paul (Bea) Dietz, was the leader of her daughter Tina's troop at Campus School. Mrs. Schwanzle's first love was camping, and during her years of Scouting, she served on established camp and day camp staffs, helped search for a campsite, and was the first camp development chairman of the Council.

Her greatest thrill was the purchase of Camp Ehawee, guiding its development, and then having her grandchild, Tina, as camper for the first time in 1959. Tina followed in her grandmother's footsteps, serving on the junior camp committee.

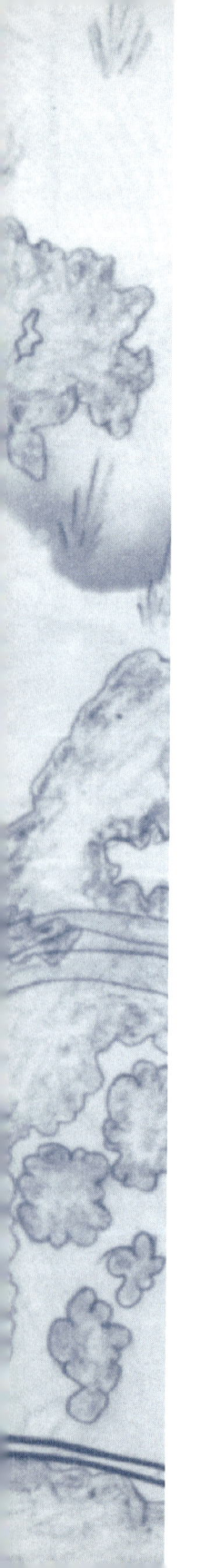

Celebrating at Camp Ehawee: Fifty Years Young

Camp Ehawee, "camp of laughing maidens," is located twenty-five miles north of La Crosse near Mindoro, Wisconsin. Purchased in 1951, it is situated on 305 acres of pine and hardwood forests near the Black River. Two nature trails, a heated swimming pool, canoe area, sports and games fields, art and nature center, central program and dining lodge, camp office, softball fields, staff program areas, and health center complete the facilities. Girls sleep in platform tents that sleep four. Campers eat in the Hope Lodge or cook meals over open fires. All living units have flush toilet facilities. Every camper participates in swimming, arts and crafts, campfires, hikes, nature activities, canoe lessons, cookouts, field games, and all camp activities. Camp Ehawee is open to all girls.

The camp is nationally accredited by the American Camping Association, a private, nonprofit educational association. This means that Riverland Council has voluntarily invited an outside team of visitors trained by ACA to verify compliance with standards in the areas of site, administration, transportation, personnel, program, health care, aquatics, trip and travel camping, and horseback riding. You can be assured that Camp Ehawee meets industry-accepted and government recognized safety standards.

The only six La Crosse women to hold the Girl Scout Thanks Badge for service got together for the first time at camp.

Standing are Miss Bertha Shuman, Mrs. C. I. Anderson, Miss Mabel Young, and Mrs. Milan Skundberg. Seated are Mrs. Philip Schwanzle, camp development chairman, and Mrs. M. R. Birnbaum, camp chairman.

Hope Kumm and campers at Camp Ehawee resident camp in the summer of 1998.

Today's Camp Ehawee staff members are mature, responsible adults employed for their abilities, qualifications, and their desire to work with children in the out-of-doors. They participate in a ten-day training that focuses on camp skills, Girl Scout program, leadership, communication, programming, and safety. Counselors live in the tent units at a ratio of one adult per six girls.

A buffet dinner and a short program, including an introduction of all staff, begins at 4:15 p.m. on each opening camp session day. On closing days, parents and family members are invited to attend a closing campfire ceremony beginning at 4:15 p.m. Campers perform in a ceremony demonstrating activities and skills learned at camp during their stay.

The new dining and program and activity center opened its doors to resident campers this summer. In addition to dining, this facility has a new kitchen and indoor bathrooms! It also houses the camp office, Trading Post, first aid station, and performing arts area.

Camp Ehawee is celebrating fifty years of excellence this summer! Quite a few things have changed since 1951, but we still hold the values of Girl Scouting and traditions of camping strong!

POSSE COUNTY — SACAJAWEA

RIVER

MINNEHAHA

DINNING LODGE

PARKING LOT

POOL

MARINUKA

COOK OUT

COOK OUT

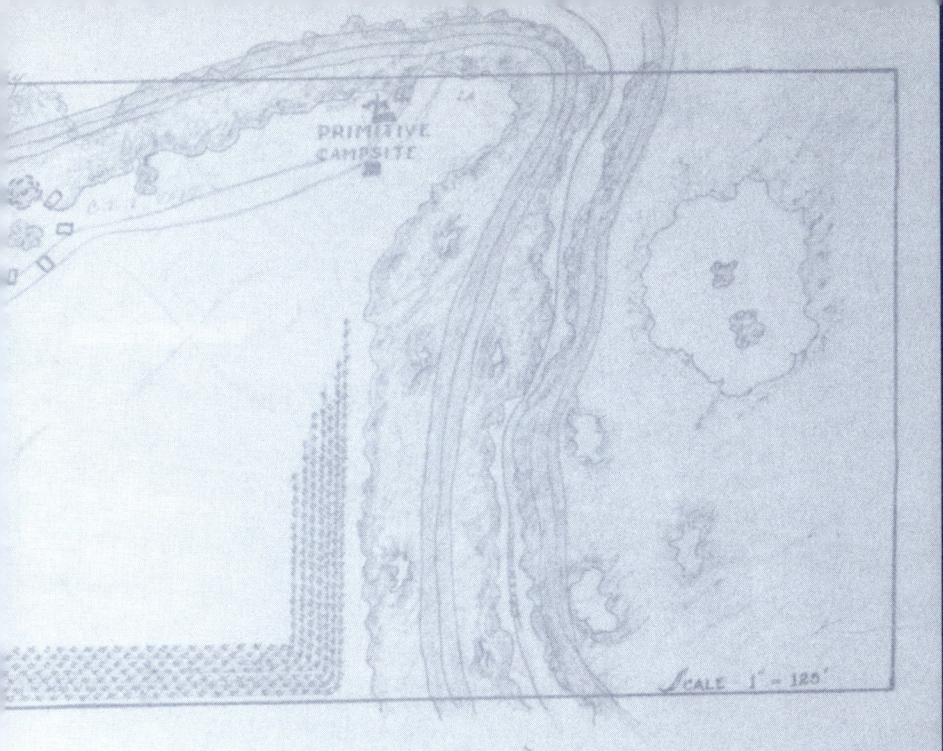

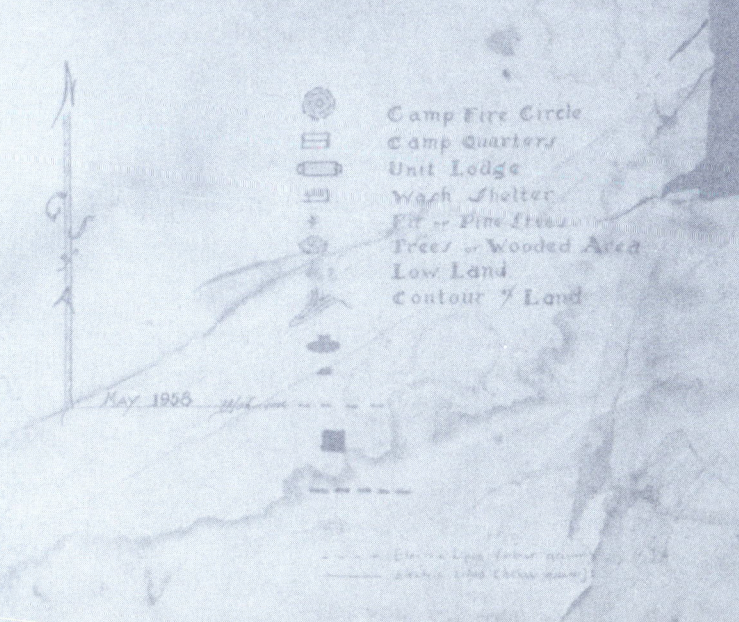

Outdoor Cooking
Recipes for the Grill or Campfire

Practical Outdoor Cooking

Our Motto: K.I.S.S. (Keep it Simple Silly!)

Cooking out is a wonderful experience for children! Here are some pointers to take the hassle out of cooking out over an open fire:

1. Have every camper search for dry kindling before attempting to light a fire. You will want a pile at least one foot high beside the fire circle before building the fire.

2. If rain is in the forecast, have campers find kindling before it rains and place under a tarp or inside a garbage bag indoors. Remember to also have dry logs in a dry place.

3. "Do as I do, not do as I say I do" when around a fire.

4. Each camper working around the fire must have hair tied back or wear a hat.

5. Have campers fill the fire bucket and bring it and a shovel or rake to the fire circle before even lighting the first match.

6. Teach as you go. When you are building the fire, talk about it with the campers. Talk about the need for a fire bucket. Talk about safety around the fire, etc.

7. Assign patrols of campers to do tasks such as food prep, keep fire going with the assistance of an adult, and cleanup. Some groups also have a patrol set the table.

8. As a general rule: if your campers are Daisies or Brownies they may collect kindling and wood, and help with food, but should not assist with fire; Juniors may do all of the above plus assisting with building the fire and adding kindling or logs to a lit fire; Cadettes and Seniors should build the fire, cook the food, add kindling and logs to the fire, and serve the adult chaperones who are watching all of this and only making comments when an action is unsafe (okay, maybe not quite to this extent!).

9. Always guess quantities of ingredients on the high side. It's much better to have too much food than not enough.

10. It's a good idea to have munchies such as carrots, ants-on-a-log (celery, peanut butter, and raisins or chocolate chips), or chips for the campers to munch on while the food is cooking.

11. Always check on campers with food allergies or vegetarian campers when planning a meal. Having a vegetarian doesn't mean that everybody has to go without meat, it just means having an alternative for that person.

12. Don't go too crazy with cooking out. Plan no more than two meals by fire a day.

13. Have peanut butter and jelly available at each cookout for the picky eaters or gals.

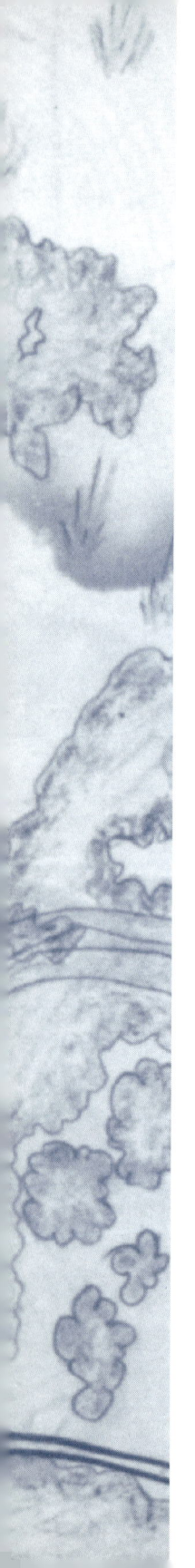

Girl Scout Cookout Checklist

The following is a checklist of equipment and supplies most easily forgotten when camping and/or cooking out! Not all of these items are a must, but this list is designed to spark a memory if forgotten. Please feel free to add your own "remember me" items.

- [ ] Garbage bags
- [ ] Paper plates or mess kits
- [ ] Aluminum foil
- [ ] Tongs
- [ ] Fire bucket
- [ ] Shovel or rake
- [ ] Bucket for heating dishwater
- [ ] Wood for the fire
- [ ] Salt and pepper
- [ ] Napkins
- [ ] Pudgy pie irons
- [ ] Can opener
- [ ] First aid kit
- [ ] Hair rubberbands
- [ ] Matches
- [ ] Kindling for fire
- [ ] Hot mitts
- [ ] Rags for dishwashing
- [ ] Dutch oven or pot
- [ ] Water cooler for juice
- [ ] Sanity!
- [ ] Dish soap
- [ ] Scrubby to clean pots
- [ ] Toilet paper

Grilled Vegetable Pizza Appetizers

1/2 (1-pound) loaf frozen bread dough, thawed, cut into halves
6 ounces shredded mozzarella cheese
6 ounces chopped tomatoes
6 ounces grilled bell peppers
4 ounces sliced mushrooms
3 ounces grilled onions
2 tablespoons chopped fresh oregano

Roll each portion of dough into a circle on a lightly floured surface. Slide each circle onto a grill rack. Grill for 1 to 2 minutes or until the bottoms begin to char. Turn over each circle.

Sprinkle with the cheese, tomatoes, bell peppers, mushrooms, onions and oregano. Grill, covered, for 1 to 2 minutes or until the crust is crisp.

Yield: 8 servings

Regional Girl Scout pioneers valued what could be learned at camp and as such established our first Girl Scout camp at Spring Banks near Sparta. Beginning in 1921, Spring Banks preceded the existence of a National Girl Scout Camp. Not until 1922 did the National Organization create Camp Andree Clark in New York.

Grilled Tomato Salad Pizza

1/2 (1-pound) loaf frozen bread
    dough, thawed
4 plum tomatoes, cut into halves
1 yellow bell pepper, quartered
1 small red onion, cut into
    1/2-inch slices
1 tablespoon olive oil
2 tablespoons light Italian salad
    dressing

2 cups chopped romaine or
    leaf lettuce
1 orange, peeled, chopped
1/4 cup sliced black olives
3 tablespoons shredded
    Parmesan cheese
2 tablespoons light Italian
    salad dressing
Freshly ground pepper to taste

Divide the dough into 8 equal portions on a lightly floured surface. Cover and let stand for 15 minutes. Roll each portion into a circle and cover.

Brush the tomatoes, bell pepper and red onion with the olive oil. Place on a vegetable grilling rack. Grill for 10 to 15 minutes or until tender, turning occasionally. Cool the vegetables slightly and cut into medium pieces.

Arrange the dough circles on a grill rack. Grill on each side for 2 to 3 minutes or until the bottom begins to char, turning once. Remove from the grill to cool. Brush with 2 tablespoons salad dressing.

Combine the vegetables, romaine, orange and olives in a large bowl and toss to mix. Arrange on the prepared crusts. Sprinkle with the Parmesan cheese. Drizzle with 2 tablespoons salad dressing. Sprinkle with pepper.

Yield: 8 servings

Camp is where girls grow strong and where outdoor programs for youth strengthen our community.

Pizza Pudgy Pies

Pudgy pies are the absolute favorite menu item at Camp Ehawee. Pudgy pies don't stop with pizza. Anything can be made in a pudgy pie iron. Try making peanut butter and jelly, grilled cheese or turkey and cheese sandwiches, desserts, etc. Desserts are made using pie filling. Yum!

1 cup (2 sticks) butter
36 slices bread
4 cups pizza sauce
8 ounces bulk sausage, cooked, drained
90 slices pepperoni
2 (4-ounce) cans sliced mushrooms, drained
4 cups shredded mozzarella cheese

Heat the irons in the fire until hot enough to melt butter. Take the irons to a food preparation bench or table. Add a small amount of butter to each side of the irons and move the butter around until both sides are coated. Lay 1 slice of bread on each side of the iron. Coat each slice of bread with pizza sauce. Add the sausage, pepperoni, mushrooms and cheese.

Close each iron carefully and clip the ends. Arrange on the coals of the fire. Have each camper watch the irons closely. We call it "look, turn, look, turn." To look, the camper will need to take the iron out of the fire, unclip the handles, open the iron and look at the color of the bread. When one side is golden brown, turn to the other side. When both sides are golden brown remove from the fire. Cool slightly and enjoy.

Yield: 18 pudgy pies

Note: Pudgy pie irons get very hot in a fire. Remind campers continuously to hold the iron down towards the ground when carrying it. It's a good idea to have campers yell "hot iron" when walking around with their hot irons. The first pudgy pie made in each iron will take longer. Watch closely so as not to burn.

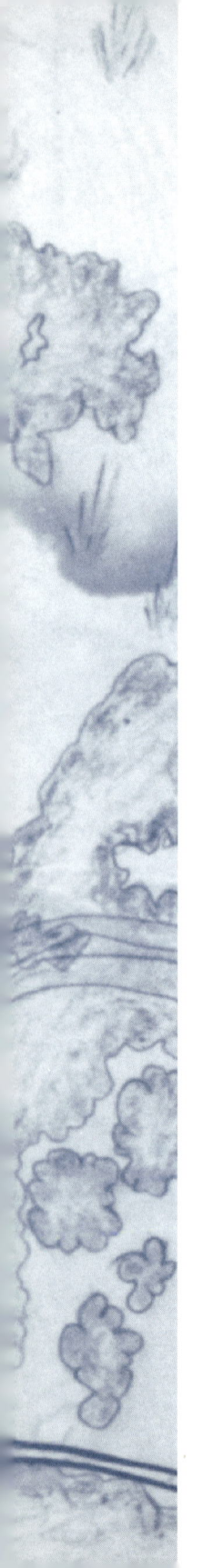

Outdoor Omelets

2 eggs
2 tablespoons shredded cheese
Crumbled cooked bacon or ham bits to taste
Chopped onions to taste
Chopped mushrooms to taste

Bring water to a boil in a large stockpot over hot coals. Crack the eggs into a sandwich-size zippered food storage bag, discarding the shells. Add the cheese, bacon, onions and mushrooms to taste. Remove the air from the bag and seal. Squish the bag to scramble the eggs.

Submerge the bag in the boiling water making sure the bag does not touch the top rim of the stockpot to prevent the bag from melting. Boil for 5 minutes or until the eggs are set. Remove the bag from the water. Unseal the bag and pour onto a serving plate.

Yield: 1 serving

Camp encompasses the best in Girl Scouting. It's a place where adventure, learning, friendships, and fun converge in a safe and supportive environment.

Grilled Sauerbraten Steak

1/4 cup red wine vinegar or cider vinegar
1/4 cup red wine
2 tablespoons water
1 1/2 tablespoons sugar
1 1/2 teaspoons salt
1/4 teaspoon onion powder
1/4 teaspoon garlic powder
1/4 teaspoon pepper
4 (6-ounce) sirloin, bison or beef steaks

Combine the vinegar, red wine, water, sugar, salt, onion powder, garlic powder and pepper in a sealable plastic food storage bag. Add the steaks and seal the bag.

Marinate for 1 hour. Drain the steaks, discarding the marinade. Arrange on a grill rack. Grill on each side over hot coals for 4 to 5 minutes or to the desired degree of doneness.

Yield: 4 servings

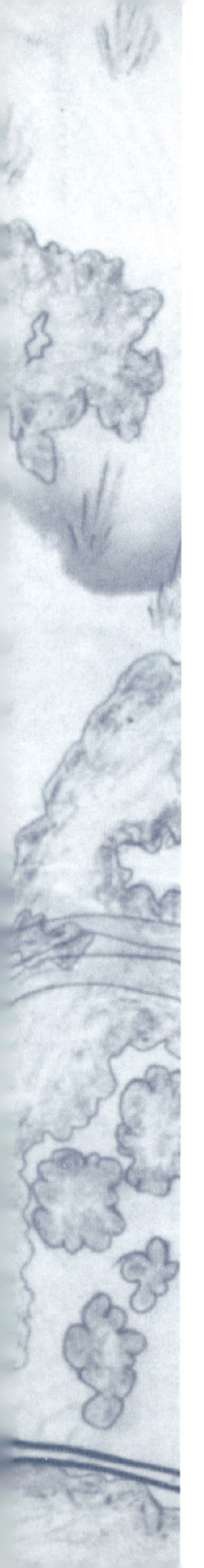

Enchilada Pie

1 pound ground beef
1 (28-ounce) jar salsa
12 large flour tortillas
8 ounces cream cheese, softened
1 pound Cheddar cheese, shredded

Brown the ground beef in a Dutch oven or large heavy saucepan over hot coals, stirring until crumbly; drain. Add 1/4 cup of the salsa and mix well. Spread each tortilla with cream cheese.

Alternate layers of the tortillas and Cheddar cheese over the ground beef mixture until all ingredients are used, ending with the Cheddar cheese. Pour the remaining salsa over the top. Cover the Dutch oven. Arrange in the hot coals, placing a shovel of coals on the top. Bake for 20 to 30 minutes or until heated through.

Yield: 6 servings

Camp is a learning environment where youth explore new challenges without the pressure of competition or risk of failure.

Mock Enchiladas

5 pounds ground beef or turkey
5 envelopes taco seasoning mix
1 cup water
2 (12-ounce) packages corn chips
2 heads lettuce, chopped
4 cups shredded Cheddar cheese
2 cups sour cream
4 tomatoes, chopped
1 (4-ounce) can sliced black olives, drained

Brown the ground beef in a Dutch oven or large heavy saucepan over hot coals; drain. Add the taco seasoning mix and water and mix well. Cook until reduced to the desired consistency, stirring constantly with a long-handled spoon. Remove from the hot coals.

To serve, instruct the campers to layer the corn chips, ground beef mixture, lettuce, cheese, sour cream, tomatoes and olives as desired on their plates.

Yield: 12 servings

Note: To serve 6, reduce all of the ingredients by half except the olives. You will still need to use 1 can of olives. To serve 24, double all of the ingredients except the lettuce. Use only 3 heads of lettuce.

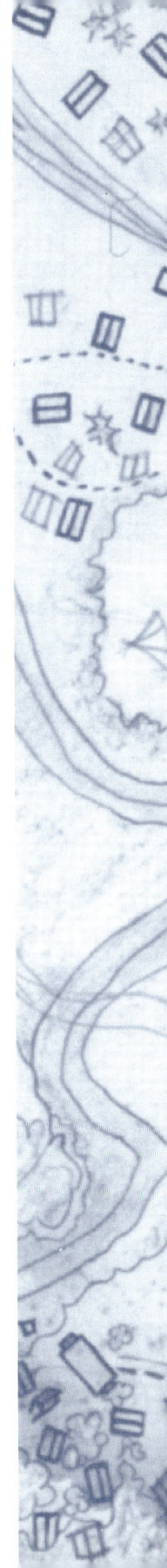

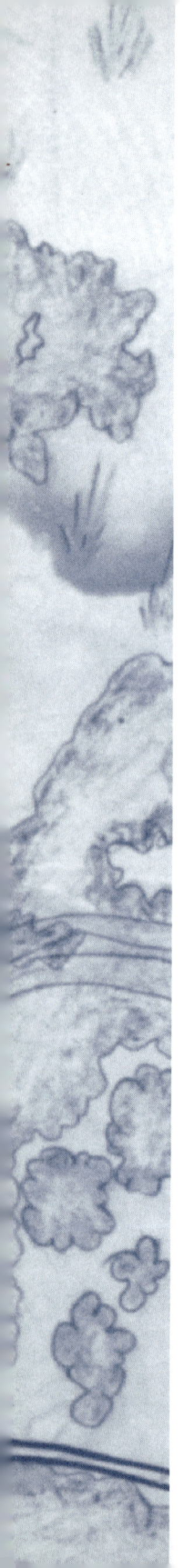

Grilled Pork Tenderloin

1/2 cup vegetable oil
1/3 cup soy sauce
1/4 cup red wine vinegar
3 tablespoons lemon juice
2 tablespoons Worcestershire sauce
1 garlic clove, crushed
1 tablespoon chopped fresh parsley
1 tablespoon dry mustard
1 1/2 teaspoons pepper
2 (12- to 16-ounce) pork tenderloins

Combine the oil, soy sauce, vinegar, lemon juice, Worcestershire sauce, garlic, parsley, dry mustard and pepper in a sealable plastic food storage bag. Add the pork and seal the bag. Turn to coat the pork well.

Marinate in the refrigerator for 4 hours. Drain the pork, discarding the marinade. Arrange on a grill rack. Grill, covered, at 300 to 400 degrees for 12 to 14 minutes or until cooked through, turning once.

Yield: 4 servings

Camp is both an outdoor classroom and laboratory, where you make new friends, increase self confidence, try out leadership skills, learn self sufficiency, and make independent decisions.

Lamb Kabobs with Couscous

12 ounces trimmed boneless lamb loin chops
1 zucchini, cut into halves lengthwise
1 yellow squash, cut into halves lengthwise
1 red bell pepper
1 tablespoon lemon juice
3 tablespoons water
1 1/2 teaspoons cumin
1 1/2 teaspoons paprika
1 teaspoon olive oil
1/2 teaspoon cinnamon
1/2 teaspoon sugar
1/4 teaspoon pepper
1 lemon, cut into 8 wedges
1 1/4 cups couscous
1/4 teaspoon salt
2 1/2 cups boiling water

Cut the lamb, zucchini, squash and bell pepper each into 16 pieces. Mix the lemon juice, 3 tablespoons water, cumin, paprika, olive oil, cinnamon, sugar and pepper in a large bowl. Add the lamb, zucchini, squash and bell pepper pieces and toss to coat.

Thread the lamb and vegetables alternately onto 8 skewers, ending with 1 lemon wedge per skewer. Arrange on a grill rack. Grill, covered, for 12 minutes or until the lamb is cooked through, turning occasionally.

Combine the couscous, salt and 2 1/2 cups boiling water in a bowl and mix well. Let stand, covered, for 5 minutes or until the liquid is absorbed. Fluff the couscous with a fork. Spoon onto a serving platter. Arrange the kabobs over the couscous and serve.

Yield: 4 servings

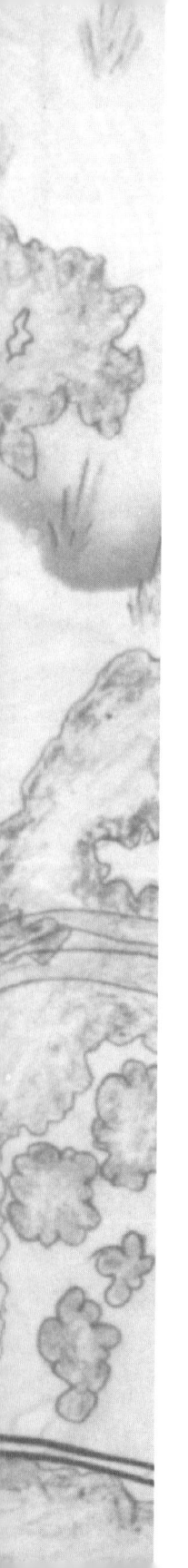

Chicken in the Woods

3 pounds boneless skinless chicken breasts
16 cups water
4 chicken bouillon cubes or to taste
1 tablespoon butter
1 pound carrots, sliced
2 cups sliced celery
12 cups instant dry rice

Cut the chicken into bite-size pieces. Sauté in a Dutch oven or large stockpot over hot coals until cooked through. Add the water, bouillon cubes, butter, carrots and celery.

Cook until the vegetables are tender. Add the rice. Cook until rice is tender.

Yield: 12 servings

Note: To serve 6, reduce all of the ingredients by half except the butter. You will still need to use 1 tablespoon of butter. To serve 24, double all of the ingredients except the butter. You will still need to use 1 tablespoon of butter.

Grilled Smoked Turkey Quesadillas

1 ounce shredded smoked turkey breast
3/4 cup shredded provolone cheese,
 or other favorite cheese
1 ounce grilled red, yellow or green bell pepper,
 or hot pepper
1 ounce grilled onion
2 (10-inch) flour tortillas
1 tablespoon light sour cream
1 tablespoon salsa

Sprinkle the turkey, cheese, bell pepper and onion onto 1 of the flour tortillas. Top with the remaining tortilla. Arrange on a grill rack.

Grill on each side for 1 to 2 minutes or until heated through. Remove from the grill rack and cut into quarters. Top each with the sour cream and salsa.

Yield: 2 servings

Camp is where youth focus on building relationships with peers and with caring, supportive adult mentors.

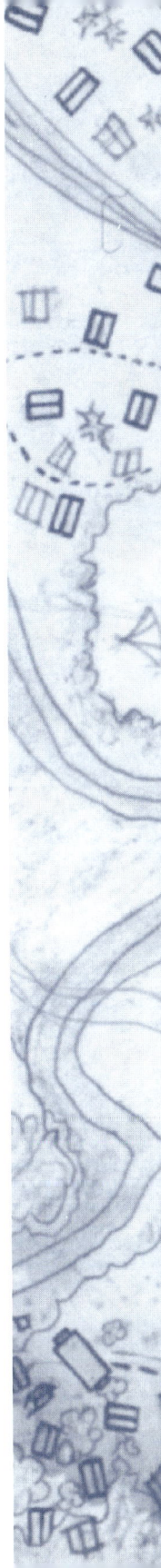

Lemon and Herb Grilled Trout

2 (8- to 16-ounce) whole trout, cleaned
1 tablespoon butter, melted
2 teaspoons Southern-Style Barbecue Rub (below)
4 lemon slices
4 fresh herb sprigs, such as parsley, basil,
  dill or your favorite herb

Rinse the trout and pat dry with a clean towel. Rub the trout inside and out with the butter. Sprinkle inside and out with the Southern-Style Barbecue Rub. Insert the lemon slices and herb sprigs inside the cavity.

Arrange in a grilling basket. Grill on each side over medium heat for 4 to 5 minutes or until the fish flakes easily.

Yield: 2 servings

Southern-Style Barbecue Rub

1/4 cup paprika
2 tablespoons salt
2 tablespoons black pepper
2 tablespoons sugar
2 tablespoons brown sugar
2 tablespoons cumin
2 tablespoons chili powder
1 tablespoon cayenne pepper

Process the paprika, salt, black pepper, sugar, brown sugar, cumin, chili powder and cayenne pepper in a blender until blended. Store in an airtight container.

Yield: about 1 cup

Grilled Marinated Walleye

2 (6-ounce) walleye fillets or other favorite fish
Seafood Marinade (below)

Arrange the fish in a shallow dish. Add the Seafood Marinade. Marinate, covered, for 30 minutes. Drain the fish, discarding the marinade.

Arrange the fish on a sheet of heavy-duty foil. Fold and seal the foil to enclose the fish. Place on a grill rack. Grill over hot coals for 10 to 15 minutes or until the fish flakes easily.

Yield: 2 servings

Seafood Marinade

1/4 cup white wine
1 tablespoon olive oil
1/2 tablespoon lemon juice
1 tablespoon grated orange zest
1 teaspoon chopped fresh ginger

1/2 teaspoon chopped chives
1/2 teaspoon dill
1 teaspoon salt
1/2 teaspoon pepper

Process the wine, olive oil, lemon juice, orange zest, ginger, chives, dill, salt and pepper in a food processor until blended.

Yield: 1/2 cup

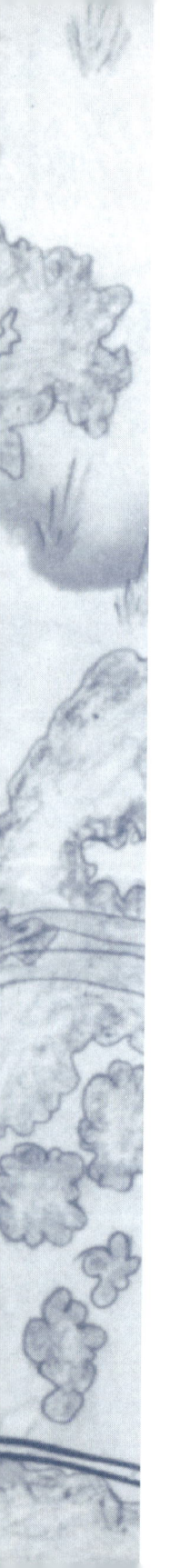

Barbecued Shrimp

1 teaspoon cayenne pepper
1 teaspoon black pepper
1/2 teaspoon salt
1/2 teaspoon crushed red pepper
1/2 teaspoon thyme
1/2 teaspoon crushed rosemary
1/8 teaspoon oregano

1 cup olive oil
2 tablespoons minced garlic
   (optional)
1 teaspoon Worcestershire sauce
2 pinches of saffron
2 pounds uncooked shrimp, peeled, deveined

Combine the cayenne pepper, black pepper, salt, red pepper, thyme, rosemary, oregano, olive oil, garlic, Worcestershire sauce and saffron in a large bowl and mix well. Add the shrimp.

Marinate, covered, in the refrigerator for 2 to 3 hours. Drain the shrimp, discarding the marinade. Arrange the shrimp on skewers. Grill over hot coals until the shrimp turn pink.

Yield: 4 servings

Stuffed. In 1980, that is how anyone who entered the Girl Scout Office would have described the conditions. There was no place to sit, let alone provide any programs for girl members. To solve the problem, Girl Scout staff members and dedicated volunteers worked together to ask the community for a state-of-the-art Girl Scout Service Center. In 1980, the dream came true with the construction of the Riverland Council Service Center by Hixon Forest in La Crosse. Today Girl Scouts use the building daily to provide badge workshops, teach leaders new skills, and provide a place for all Girl Scouts.

Pioneer Beans

1 pound ground beef
1 (28-ounce) can baked beans
1 (14-ounce) can butter beans
1 (14-ounce) can kidney beans
1 (14-ounce) can navy beans
1/3 cup packed brown sugar
2 to 3 tablespoons prepared mustard
2 to 3 tablespoons ketchup
1 to 2 tablespoons molasses

Brown the ground beef in a 10- to 12-inch Dutch oven over hot coals, stirring until crumbly; drain. Add the baked beans, butter beans, kidney beans, navy beans, brown sugar, mustard, ketchup and molasses and mix well.

Cover the Dutch oven with the lid. Place a shovel of coals over the lid. Bake for 20 to 30 minutes or until heated through.

Yield: 6 to 8 servings

Note: You may use ham or bacon instead of the ground beef.

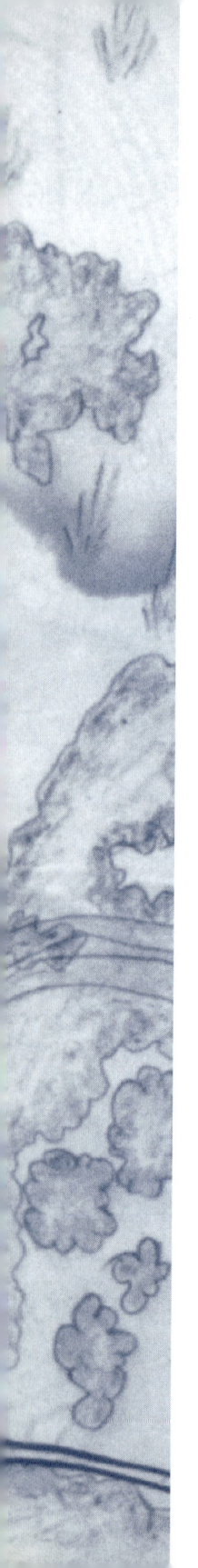

Campfire Potatoes

5 medium potatoes, peeled, thinly sliced
1 medium onion, sliced
6 tablespoons butter or margarine
1/3 cup shredded Cheddar cheese
2 tablespoons minced parsley
1 tablespoon Worcestershire sauce
Salt and pepper to taste
1/3 cup chicken broth

Arrange the potatoes and onion on a 20×20-inch piece of heavy-duty foil. Dot with the butter. Mix the cheese, parsley, Worcestershire sauce, salt and pepper in a bowl. Sprinkle over the potatoes.

Fold the foil up around the potato mixture. Add the broth. Seal the foil edges to enclose the potato mixture. Arrange on a grill rack. Grill, covered, over medium heat for 35 to 40 minutes or until the potatoes are tender.

Yield: 4 to 6 servings

Playing practical jokes at camp is a long-standing tradition for both campers of today and yesterday. Early one morning at camp, one staff member recalls how she played a joke on the whole camp. "A note was left on the kitchen table that read, 'They have taken us—Save us!' The alarm was sounded and everyone searched every nook and corner. Then, someone saw a few scattered pieces of paper that gave directions to a place just over the hill. The campers climbed the hill, crossed the meadow, and found a wooded area just beyond, where breakfast was prepared for all of camp."

Outdoor Vegetables

4 red potatoes, quartered
3 carrots, sliced
4 to 7 fresh mushrooms, sliced
1/2 large green bell pepper, sliced
1 onion, sliced
1 teaspoon minced garlic
1 (10-ounce) can cream of chicken or mushroom soup
1/4 to 1/2 cup (1/2 to 1 stick) butter or margarine

Combine the potatoes, carrots, mushrooms, bell pepper, onion and garlic in a bowl and toss to mix well. Divide the vegetable mixture into 2 equal portions. Arrange each portion on a large piece of heavy-duty foil. Top with the soup and butter.

Fold each piece of foil to enclose the vegetable mixture. Wrap each packet twice with foil. Place on a grill rack. Grill for 45 to 60 minutes or until the vegetables are cooked through.

Yield: 4 to 6 servings

Note: You may use your favorite vegetables and substitute cheese soup for the cream of chicken soup.

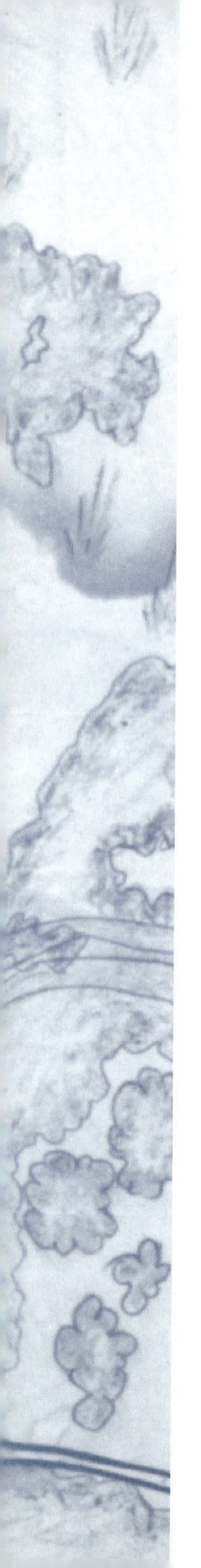

Angels on Horseback

1/2 cup (1 stick) butter
6 cups baking mix
Water
1 cup packed brown sugar
1 cup sugar

Melt the butter in a small saucepan. Mix the baking mix with enough water in a bowl to form a sticky dough. Have each camper find a stick as big around as her pinky finger and as long as her arm. Give each camper a small handful of dough. Let each camper wrap the dough around the top end of her stick. Hold the sticks over the hot coals.

Bake until the dough on the end of each stick turns a golden brown. Remove immediately from the heat. Dip into the melted butter. Roll in a mixture of the brown sugar and sugar.

Yield: 12 servings

Note: To serve 6, reduce all of the ingredients by half except the butter. You will still need to use 1/2 cup butter. To serve 24, double all of the ingredients.

Camp serves many purposes for the children of Riverland Council. Early in its beginning, campers came from near and far to experience nature. To expand the opportunity for Girl Scouts, Day Camp was created in 1932. Beginning at Onalaska Park, Riverland Council now offers ten day camps serving over 1000 girls and adult volunteers each year.

Banana Boats

12 bananas
24 large marshmallows
2 cups (12 ounces) chocolate chips

Cut each unpeeled banana lengthwise 3/4 through. Tear apart the marshmallows and stuff inside each banana. Sprinkle with the chocolate chips. Wrap each stuffed banana tightly in 1 layer of heavy-duty foil.

Arrange in the hot coals. Grill until the marshmallows and chocolate chips are melted, checking each packet once or twice. Remove from the coals and unwrap carefully. Eat the banana boats directly from the peels.

Yield: 12 servings

Haystackers

2 cups (4 sticks) butter
2 (10-ounce) packages marshmallows
3 cups (18 ounces) chocolate chips
2 cups peanut butter (optional)
12 cups cornflakes

Melt the butter and marshmallows in a Dutch oven or large stockpot over hot coals, stirring constantly with a long-handled spoon. Remove from the heat. Add the chocolate chips and peanut butter and stir constantly until smooth. Add the cornflakes and mix well. Spoon onto each camper's serving plate.

Yield: 12 servings

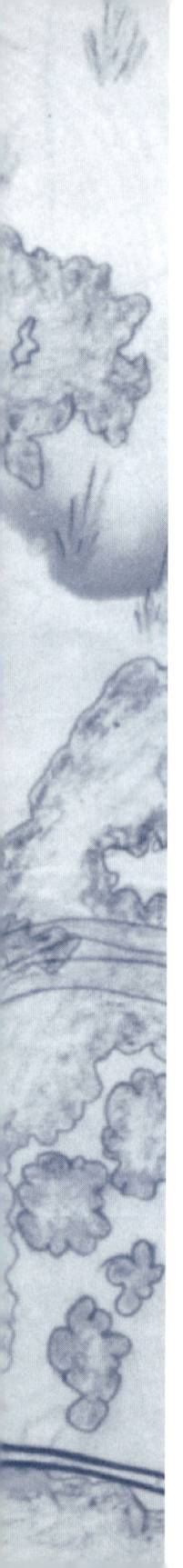

Shaggy Dogs

1 1/2 cups (9 ounces) chocolate chips
12 marshmallows
4 cups crisp rice cereal or shredded coconut

Melt the chocolate chips in a small saucepan over hot coals. Place each marshmallow on a wooden pick. Roll each in the melted chocolate first. Then roll in the cereal until coated.

Yield: 12 servings

Note: To serve 6, reduce all of the ingredients by half except the chocolate chips. Use 1 cup chocolate chips. To serve 24, double all of the ingredients except the chocolate chips. Use 2 cups chocolate chips.

Campfire Cobbler

2 (16-ounce) cans apple, peach or cherry pie filling
1 (2-layer) package yellow cake mix
1 envelope maple and brown sugar instant oats

Lightly oil a 10- or 12-inch Dutch oven and line with foil. Spread the pie filling in the prepared Dutch oven. Cover with the dry cake mix. Sprinkle with the instant oats. Cover the Dutch oven.

Arrange in the hot coals, placing a shovel of coals on the top. Bake for 1 hour.

Yield: 8 servings

Alabama Pudding

2 (20-ounce) cans applesauce
1 package gingerbread mix
8 ounces whipped topping

Bring the applesauce to a boil in a Dutch oven over hot coals. Prepare the gingerbread mix using the package directions. Spoon the gingerbread batter over the hot applesauce. Cover the Dutch oven. Arrange in the hot coals, placing a shovel of coals on the top. Bake for 25 to 30 minutes. Serve with the whipped topping.

Down by the Creek

In memory of Virginia Hoffland, who was a devoted Girl Scout Leader for Troop #123 of Soldiers Grove.

One memorable night in 1965 on the banks of a creek on Virginia's farm, we set up our tents, dug the latrine and started a campfire. Supper consisted of campfire stew, pigs-in-a-blanket and Alabama Pudding. For a midnight snack we made s'mores and popped popcorn over the campfire. I remember waking to the song of a whippoorwill the next morning. For breakfast we had bacon, eggs and baked beans we baked underground. After breakfast we cleaned up camp and I went home with memories of my first Girl Scout camping trip on the banks of Trout Creek.

Bonnie Young
Soldiers Grove, Wisconsin

SACAJAWEA

MINNEHAHA

DINNING LODGE

PARKING LOT

POOL

MARINUKA

COOK OUT

COOK OUT

Healthy Nibbles
Appetizers and Snacks

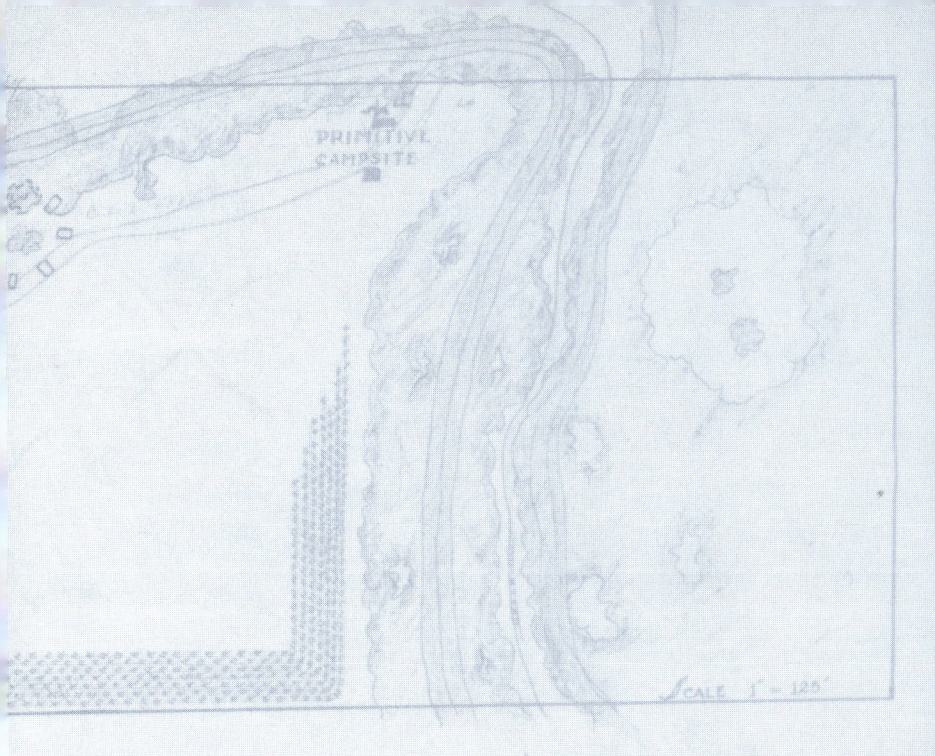

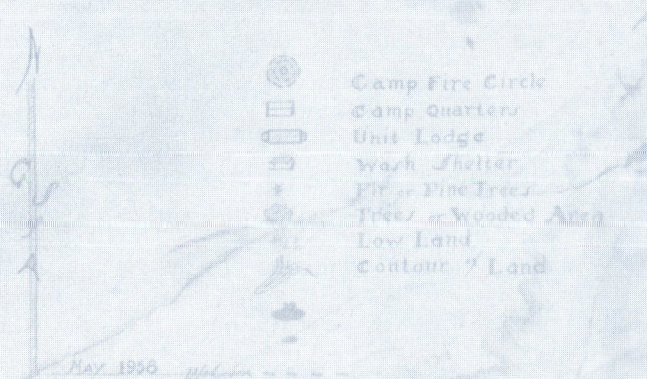

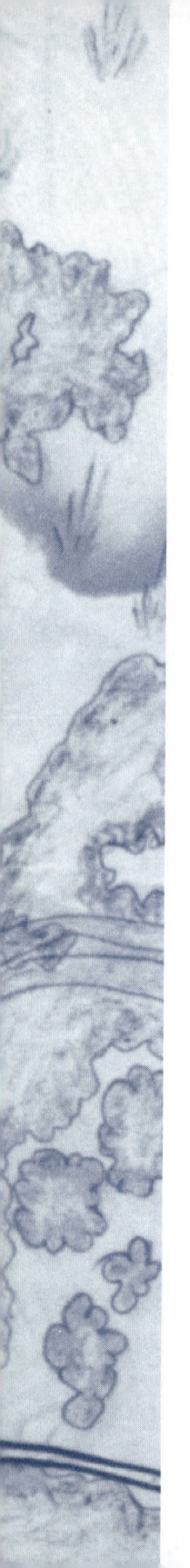

Caramel Apple Dip

8 ounces cream cheese, softened
1 cup dry roasted peanuts, chopped
3/4 cup packed brown sugar
1/4 cup sugar
2 teaspoons vanilla extract

Process the cream cheese, peanuts, brown sugar, sugar and vanilla in a food processor or blender until smooth. Serve with apple wedges.

Yield: 2 cups

Pretzel Dip

1/2 cup dry mustard
1/2 cup white vinegar
1 egg
1/2 cup sugar
Dash of salt
1 cup nonfat mayonnaise

Mix the dry mustard and vinegar in a bowl. Chill, covered, for 8 to 12 hours. Beat the egg, sugar and salt in a double boiler until smooth. Add the mustard mixture. Cook over hot water until the mixture coats a spoon. Remove from the heat to cool. Add the mayonnaise and mix well. Store, covered, in the refrigerator. Serve with pretzels.

Yield: 3 cups

Seven-Layer Southwestern Dip

1 (15-ounce) can black beans
1 (8-ounce) jar chunky salsa
1/2 cup chopped red bell pepper
1/4 cup sliced green onions
3 cups shredded lettuce
1 cup light sour cream
2 jalapeño chiles, minced (optional)
1 teaspoon grated lime zest
1/2 medium avocado, peeled, coarsely chopped
2/3 cup shredded Cheddar cheese
1/3 cup chopped pitted black olives
1 tablespoon snipped fresh cilantro

Rinse the black beans and drain. Drain any excess liquid from the salsa. Mix the black beans, bell pepper and green onions in a bowl. Line a 12-inch platter with the shredded lettuce. Spoon the black bean mixture onto the lettuce to within 1 inch of the edge. Spread the sour cream over the black bean mixture. Sprinkle with the chiles and lime zest. Mix the salsa and avocado in a bowl. Spread over the top. Sprinkle with the cheese, olives and cilantro.

Yield: 32 servings

Spicy Vegetable Dip

1 cup mayonnaise-type salad dressing
1/2 cup sour cream
1 tablespoon onion powder
1/2 tablespoon garlic salt
1/4 teaspoon paprika
1/2 tablespoon lemon juice
1/2 teaspoon Worcestershire sauce

Combine the salad dressing, sour cream, onion powder, garlic salt, paprika, lemon juice and Worcestershire sauce in a bowl and mix well. Chill, covered, in the refrigerator. Serve with bite-size fresh vegetables.

Yield: 1 1/2 cups

Garlic Breadsticks

1 cup all-purpose flour
2 teaspoons garlic powder
1 envelope dry yeast
2/3 cup warm water
1 tablespoon sugar

1 teaspoon salt
1/4 cup vegetable oil
1 cup all-purpose flour
1 egg, beaten
Salt to taste

Sift 1 cup flour and garlic powder together. Dissolve the yeast in the warm water. Stir in the sugar, 1 teaspoon salt and oil Beat in the flour mixture until smooth. Add 1 cup flour. Knead for 5 minutes or until smooth. Let rise, covered, until doubled in bulk. Divide the dough into two equal portions. Cut each portion into twenty-four pieces. Roll each piece into long sticks. Arrange on a greased baking sheet. Brush with the beaten egg. Sprinkle with salt to taste. Bake at 350 degrees for 15 to 20 minutes or until brown. Turn off the oven. Let stand in the oven for 1 1/2 hours.

Yield: 48 breadsticks

Swannie's Orange Honey Muffins

1 cup all-purpose flour
1 tablespoon baking powder
1/2 teaspoon salt
1/2 teaspoon baking soda
1 cup rolled oats
1 tablespoon wheat germ

1 cup orange juice
1/3 cup honey
1 egg
3 tablespoons vegetable oil
1 tablespoon grated orange zest

Combine all the ingredients in a large bowl and mix well. Spoon into greased muffin cups, filling 3/4 full. Bake at 375 degrees for 25 to 35 minutes or until the muffins test done.

Yield: 1 dozen

My mother, Marie Schwanzle or "Swannie," was chairwoman of the Girl Scout Camp Development Committee. Every weekend for several years, she and daddy would take off with members of the committee in search of property suitable for a new Girl Scout camp. Among those members were the late Orville Hayes, Carl and Helen Schubert, the Milan Skundbergs, Hope Kumm, and many others. The requirements set by the National Girl Scouts were stringent. They hiked over one prospective farm after another only to find that each lacked a particular qualification. Finally they found the property in Mindoro and they were elated.

It was, as I think back, one of the happiest times of their lives. They spent their weekends planting the seedling pines that now, fifty years later, add to the beauty of Camp Ehawee.

I can remember the excitement surrounding the "name the camp contest." Ehawee means "laughing maidens" in Native American and that provided the theme for naming the camp units.

The "Do-Dads," as they called themselves, were a group of fathers and grandfathers of Girl Scouts who would volunteer their weekend to painting, repairing, and building projects to ready the camp for its opening. Mother was awarded the Thanks Badge for her years of service to the Girl Scouts.

Sally Cremer Williams

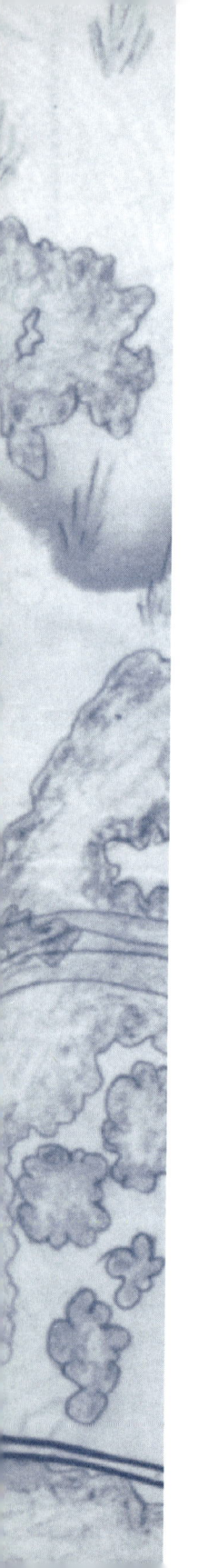

Broccoli Ham Ring

2 (8-count) cans crescent roll dough
1 1/2 cups shredded Swiss cheese
4 ounces cooked ham, chopped
2 1/4 cups chopped fresh broccoli
1 small onion, chopped
1/4 cup minced fresh parsley
2 tablespoons Dijon mustard
1 teaspoon lemon juice

Unroll the crescent roll dough and divide into triangles. Arrange in a circle on a 12-inch pizza pan with the pointed ends facing outward and the wide ends overlapping, pressing the wide ends together.

Combine the cheese, ham, broccoli, onion, parsley, Dijon mustard and lemon juice in a bowl and mix well. Spoon over the wide ends of the dough. Fold the dough points over the filling and tuck under the wide ends. The filling will still be visible. Bake at 375 degrees for 20 to 25 minutes or until golden brown.

Yield: 6 to 8 servings

From its beginning in Savannah, Georgia, Girl Scouting quickly spread through the nation—and Southwestern Wisconsin is among the first to call Girl Scouting home. Community groups in the La Crosse area rounded up a committee and founded Girl Scout troop #1 led by Mrs. J. E. McConnel in 1917. Today the Girl Scouts of Riverland Council proudly charter more than 500 Girl Scout troops reaching over 4000 girls.

Chicken Tortilla Roll-ups

3 tablespoons reduced-fat cream cheese, softened
2 tablespoons salsa
1 tablespoon reduced-fat sour cream
2 flour tortillas
2 lettuce leaves
2 tablespoons red and/or yellow bell pepper strips
2 tablespoons thin carrot strips
1/4 cup chopped cooked chicken
2 tablespoons raisins, chopped

Combine the cream cheese, salsa and sour cream in a bowl and blend well. Spread on the tortillas. Layer the lettuce leaves, bell pepper strips, carrot strips, chicken and raisins on top. Roll up to enclose the filling. Cut crosswise to form pinwheels. Serve with additional salsa.

Yield: 12 pinwheels

Note: Use your favorite lean meat and vegetables of choice. Try using Dijon mustard instead of the salsa.

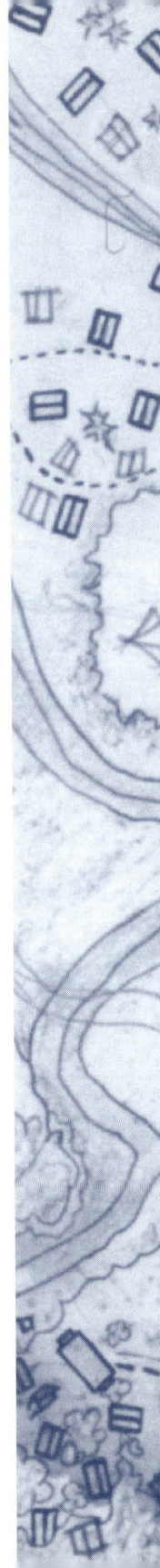

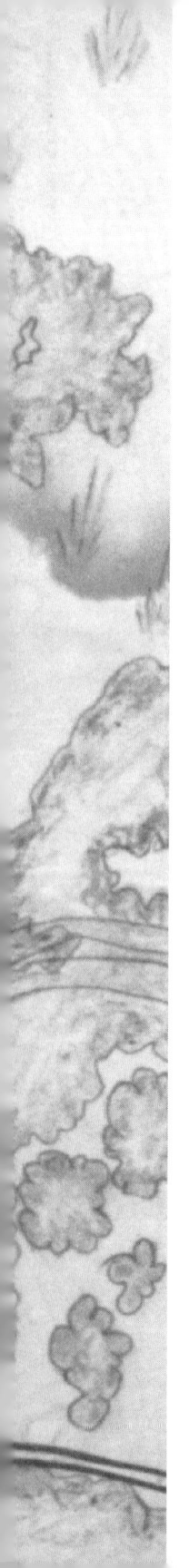

Ham Pickle Spears

8 ounces cream cheese, softened
8 ham slices
8 Claussen pickle spears, drained

Spread the cream cheese evenly over each ham slice. Place a pickle spear at the end of each ham slice. Roll up to enclose the pickle spear and secure with a wooden pick. Cut into bite-size pieces.

Yield: 8 servings

Miniature Pita Pizza

1 miniature pita bread round
1 tablespoon pizza or pasta sauce
1 ounce mozzarella cheese, shredded

Arrange the pita on a baking sheet. Spread the pizza sauce evenly over the pita. Sprinkle with the cheese. Broil until the cheese melts.

Yield: 1 serving

Smoked Salmon Spread

8 ounces smoked salmon fillet
2 green onions, finely chopped
4 hard-cooked eggs, finely chopped
1 teaspoon chopped fresh parsley
Dash of lemon pepper
Dash of cayenne pepper
Dash of lemon juice
1/4 cup mayonnaise-type salad dressing

Make sure all the bones are removed from the salmon. Flake the salmon in a large bowl. Add the green onions, hard-cooked eggs, parsley, lemon pepper, cayenne pepper, lemon juice and mayonnaise-type salad dressing and mix well. Use as a sandwich spread or as a filling for tomatoes.

Yield: 4 to 6 servings

As Girl Scouting flourished nationally, it also bloomed locally. Early troops formed in La Crosse and soon spread into neighboring communities. On Valentine's Day 1925, 19 girls from West Salem joined together to form their very own Girl Scout troop. By 1926, all local Girl Scout troops were called to a Girl Scout rally to share ideas with sister Girl Scouts from all over the region.

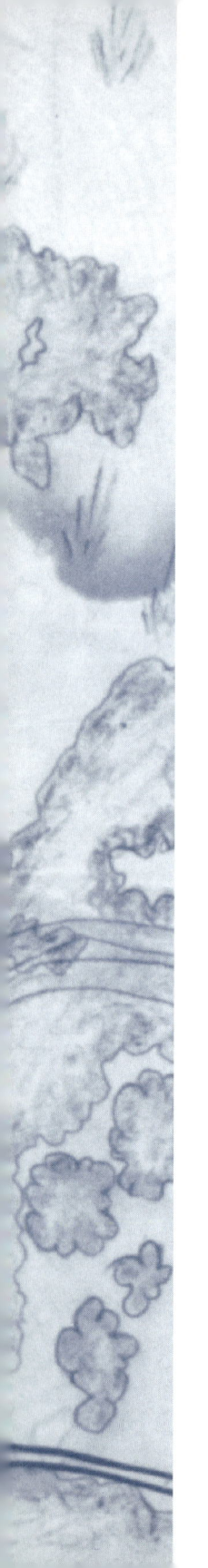

Salmon Cocktail Balls

8 ounces cream cheese, softened
1 (15-ounce) can salmon, drained, flaked
1/4 cup chopped fresh parsley
1 tablespoon lemon juice

2 tablespoons Dijon mustard
1/2 cup grated Parmesan cheese
1/2 teaspoon salt
1/4 teaspoon pepper
2 cups chopped fresh parsley

Beat the cream cheese in a medium mixing bowl until fluffy. Stir in the salmon, 1/4 cup parsley, lemon juice, Dijon mustard, Parmesan cheese, salt and pepper. Chill, covered, for 2 hours or longer. Shape into balls, using 2 teaspoons of the mixture for each ball. Dip the bottom of each ball into 2 cups parsley. Arrange parsley side down on a serving platter. Chill, covered, until serving time. Serve using wooden picks.

Yield: 5 dozen

Note: You may use three 6-ounce packages of crab meat, drained and flaked, or three 6-ounce cans of tuna, drained, instead of the salmon.

In the early days of Girl Scouting, the troop was the base for most Girl Scouts. Many troops began by using the Boy Scout Handbook until published materials arrived from the Girl Scout Headquarters. To improve the quality of Girl Scout services, the National Organization began to create councils to reach their 200,000 members. In 1930, the 250 girls and 12 troops of Southwestern Wisconsin were officially chartered as the Riverland Girl Scout Council.

Fruit Salad

1 cup reduced-fat cottage cheese
1 cup pineapple chunks
2/3 cup mandarin orange sections

Combine the cottage cheese, pineapple and mandarin oranges in a bowl and mix well. Chill, covered, until ready to serve.

Yield: 1 serving

Note: For a special presentation, layer the ingredients in a parfait glass.

Banana Fruit Kabobs

Thick banana slices
Seedless grapes
Pineapple chunks
Strawberries
Honeydew melon cubes
Cantaloupe cubes

Skewer bananas, grapes, pineapple, strawberries, honeydew melon and cantaloupe alternately on plastic drinking straws. Chill, covered, until ready to serve.

Yield: variable

Honey-Glazed Snack Mix

4 cups rice or corn Chex cereal
1 1/2 cups miniature pretzels
1 cup pecan halves

1/3 cup butter or margarine
1/4 cup honey

Combine the cereal, pretzels and pecans in a large bowl and toss to mix well. Melt the butter in a small saucepan. Add the honey. Heat until dissolved, stirring constantly. Pour over the cereal mixture and toss until evenly coated. Spread in a 10×15-inch baking pan. Bake at 350 degrees for 12 to 15 minutes or until the mixture is lightly glazed, stirring occasionally. Remove from the oven. Let stand to cool slightly. Spread the mixture on waxed paper. Let stand until completely cool.

Yield: 6 1/2 cups

Jack-O'-Lantern Jumble

1/4 cup smooth peanut butter
1/4 cup (1/2 stick) margarine
1/2 teaspoon salt
1/4 teaspoon garlic powder
2 1/4 teaspoons Worcestershire sauce

4 cups rice Chex cereal
4 cups wheat Chex cereal
3/4 cup cocktail peanuts
1 cup candy corn

Combine the peanut butter and margarine in a 10×15-inch baking pan. Bake at 250 degrees for 5 minutes or until shiny and soft. Remove from the oven. Add the salt, garlic powder and Worcestershire sauce and stir until smooth. Add the cereals and peanuts and stir until coated. Bake for 1 hour, stirring every 15 minutes. Remove from the oven. Stir in the candy. Spread on absorbent paper. Let stand until cool.

Yield: 9 cups

Oyster Cracker Snack

1/2 teaspoon onion powder
1/2 teaspoon garlic powder
1/2 teaspoon lemon pepper
1/2 teaspoon dillweed
1 envelope buttermilk ranch salad dressing mix
1 cup vegetable oil
3 (10-ounce) packages oyster crackers

Combine the onion powder, garlic powder, lemon pepper, dillweed, salad dressing mix and oil in a bowl and mix well. Let stand for 1 hour or longer, stirring with a fork frequently. Pour over the crackers in a large bowl with a lid. Replace the lid and shake well frequently. Let stand for 10 to 12 hours. Stir with a spoon before serving.

Yield: 4 cups

Yogurt Sundae

1/2 banana, peeled
2 tablespoons wheat germ, toasted
1/2 cup yogurt
Sunflower seeds or nuts

Split the banana into halves and arrange in a dessert dish. Sprinkle with the wheat germ. Top with the yogurt. Sprinkle with sunflower seeds or nuts.

Yield: 1 serving

Apple Soda

1 (16-ounce) can frozen unsweetened apple juice concentrate
6 cups carbonated or seltzer water, chilled

Thaw the apple juice concentrate. Combine the apple juice concentrate and carbonated water in a large pitcher and mix well. Pour into serving glasses.

Yield: 6 servings

Fruit Fizz

1/2 cup favorite fruit juice or nectar, chilled
1/2 cup carbonated or seltzer water, chilled

Mix the fruit juice and carbonated water in a serving glass. For a lighter drink, use 1/4 cup juice and 3/4 cup carbonated or seltzer water.

Yield: 1 serving

The original vision of Girl Scouting was to provide programming for teen and preteen girls. As more and more younger children became interested in the program a new level was added. In the 1930s, the Brownie Girl Scout level was officially adopted—and by 1936, Riverland Council had active Brownie troops. Today, Brownie Girl Scouts make up the largest population of total Girl Scouts.

Frozen Fruit Slush

1 (15-ounce) can fruit of choice

Place the can of fruit in the freezer. Freeze until firm. Defrost slightly by holding the can under running water for 1 to 2 minutes. Open the can and place the frozen fruit in a blender. Process until slushy. Pour into a serving glass and serve with a straw.

Yield: 1 serving

Lemonade

2 tablespoons lemon juice
2 teaspoons honey
1/4 cup hot water
3/4 cup cold water
Ice cubes

Combine the lemon juice, honey and hot water in a tall serving glass and mix until the honey dissolves. Add the cold water and mix well. Add ice cubes and serve.

Yield: 1 serving

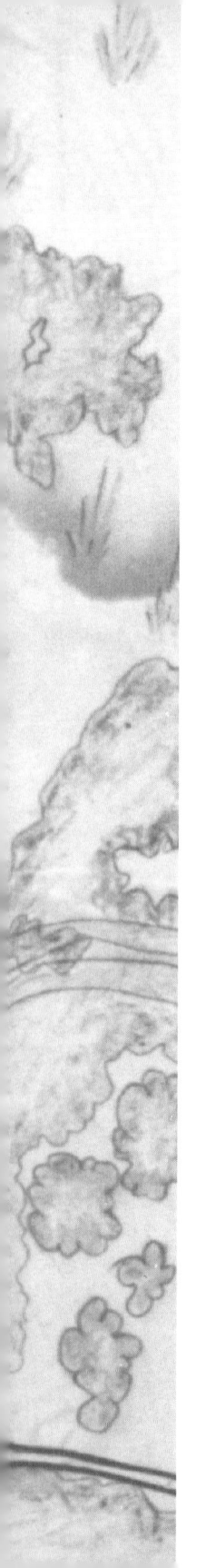

Beat-the-Heat Smoothie

8 large strawberries, frozen
1 banana, peeled
20 blueberries, frozen
3 ounces vanilla or plain yogurt
1 cup apple juice
4 ice cubes

Process the strawberries, banana, blueberries, yogurt, apple juice and ice cubes in a blender until smooth. Pour into 2 glasses. Garnish with fruit of choice.

Yield: 2 servings

Despite the wartime shortages being experienced during the 1940s, one dedicated camp director proclaimed there would be "no wartime shortages in service to youth." Troop leaders, community members, and Mrs. Marie Schwanzle forged ahead to ensure programming for girls during the summer. Myrick Park was opened for Day Camp Programming and Camp Decorah was opened to girls for a part of the summer of 1944.

Blueberry Smoothie

1 large banana
1 cup blueberries
2 cups milk or Rice Dream vanilla (rice milk)
2 tablespoons honey

Peel the banana and cut into pieces. Place on a freezer tray and cover. Freeze until firm. Process the frozen banana, blueberries, milk and honey in a blender until smooth. Pour into 2 tall serving glasses.

Yield: 2 servings

Peach Melba Smoothie

1 (16-ounce) can peaches
1/4 cup fresh or frozen raspberries
1/2 cup yogurt
3 ice cubes

Process the peaches, raspberries, yogurt and ice cubes in a blender until smooth. Pour into 2 tall serving glasses. Garnish with fruit of choice.

Yield: 2 servings

OSSE COUNTY SACAJAWEA

MINNEHAHA

DINNING LODGE

PARKING LOT

MARINUKA

POOL

COOK OUT COOK OUT

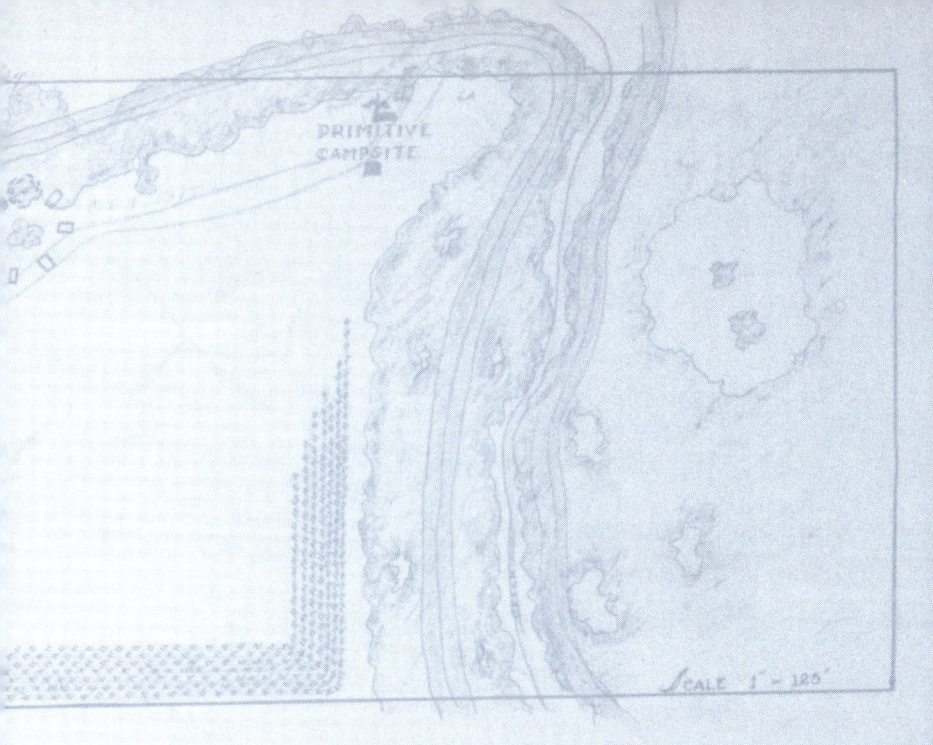

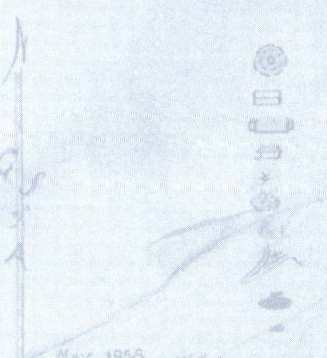

Girl Scout Greens
Salads and Side Dishes

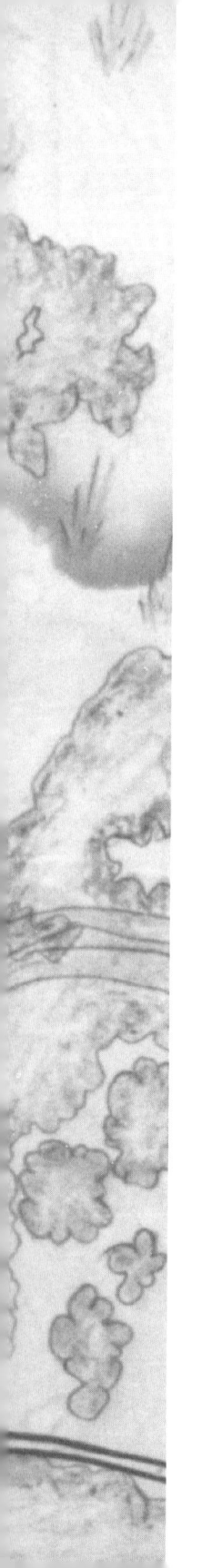

Dressing for Girl Scout Greens

1 1/2 cups vegetable juice cocktail
2 tablespoons vinegar
1 teaspoon prepared mustard
1 teaspoon Worcestershire sauce
Dash of paprika

Combine the vegetable juice cocktail, vinegar, prepared mustard, Worcestershire sauce and paprika in a jar with a tight-fitting lid. Cover the jar and shake well until blended. Serve over your favorite salad greens.

Yield: 1 1/2 cups

Raspberry Poppy Seed Vinaigrette

1/2 cup sugar
1/4 cup raspberry vinegar
1/2 cup corn oil
2 tablespoons poppy seeds
1 tablespoon sesame seeds
1 tablespoon Worcestershire sauce
1 teaspoon minced onion
1 teaspoon paprika

Combine the sugar and raspberry vinegar in a small saucepan. Heat over low heat until the sugar dissolves, whisking constantly. Remove from the heat. Whisk in the corn oil. Add the poppy seeds, sesame seeds, Worcestershire sauce, onion and paprika and whisk well. Pour into a covered container. Chill, covered, until ready to use.

Yield: 1 1/4 cups

Bok Choy Salad

2 (3-ounce) packages ramen noodles
1/2 cup (1 stick) butter
2 tablespoons sugar
3 ounces slivered almonds
1/2 cup sesame seeds

3/4 cup vegetable oil
1/2 cup sugar
1/4 cup red wine vinegar
2 tablespoons soy sauce
2 large heads bok choy, chopped
4 green onion tops, sliced

Crumble the ramen noodles and reserve the seasoning packets for another purpose. Melt the butter in a skillet. Add 2 tablespoons sugar, almonds, sesame seeds and crumbled ramen noodles. Sauté until light brown. Remove from the heat to cool.

Combine the oil, 1/2 cup sugar, red wine vinegar and soy sauce in a jar with a tight-fitting lid. Cover the jar and shake well until blended.

Combine the bok choy and green onions in a large serving bowl. Add the ramen noodle mixture and toss to mix well. Drizzle with the salad dressing and toss to coat.

Yield: 10 to 12 servings

Broccoli Salad

1 envelope Italian salad dressing mix

2 pounds broccoli florets
1 cup crumbled feta cheese

Prepare the salad dressing mix using the package directions, using balsamic vinegar. Combine the broccoli and feta cheese in a salad bowl. Add the salad dressing and toss to coat. Chill, covered, until ready to serve.

Yield: 8 servings

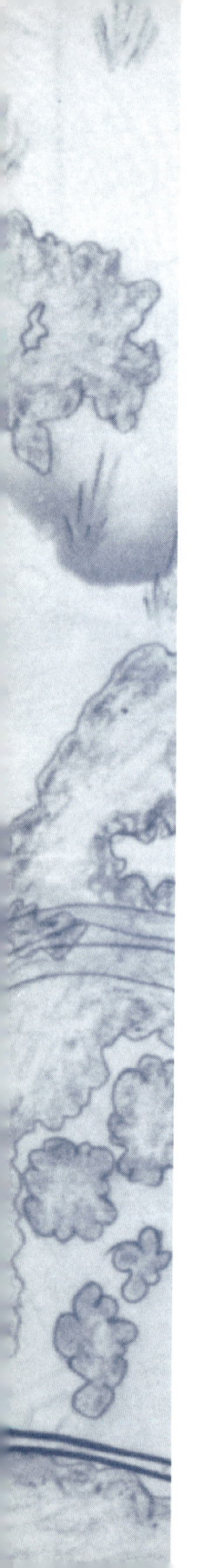

Raisin Broccoli Salad

5 cups fresh broccoli florets
1 cup raisins
8 ounces bacon, cooked, crumbled
1/2 cup cashews, sunflower seed kernels or pine nuts
Chopped red onion to taste
1/4 cup mayonnaise or mayonnaise-type salad dressing
3 to 4 tablespoons sugar
1 tablespoon vinegar

Combine the broccoli, raisins, bacon, cashews and red onion in a large serving bowl. Mix the mayonnaise, sugar and vinegar in a small bowl. Pour over the broccoli mixture and toss to coat. Chill, covered, until ready to serve.

Yield: 6 servings

Spinach and Roasted Garlic Salad

1 1/2 pounds fresh baby spinach leaves
12 garlic cloves, roasted
1/4 cup toasted almonds
3 tablespoons extra-virgin olive oil
Juice of 1/2 lemon
Salt and freshly ground pepper to taste

Place the spinach in a large salad bowl. Add the unpeeled roasted garlic and almonds. Drizzle with the olive oil and lemon juice. Season with salt and pepper and toss to coat well. Serve immediately, having everyone squeeze the softened garlic purée out of the garlic skin to eat.

Yield: 8 servings

Brown Rice Salad with Mango Salsa

1 (16-ounce) can black beans, rinsed, drained
1 1/2 cups cooked brown rice
2 ribs celery, chopped
1/2 cup sliced pimento-stuffed olives or Spanish olives
Salt and pepper to taste
1/2 cup orange juice
1 1/2 tablespoons cider vinegar
3 tablespoons olive oil
2 teaspoons grated orange zest
2 tablespoons chopped parsley
2 tablespoons chopped cilantro
1/2 cup minced green onions
2 teaspoons ground cumin
1 teaspoon cinnamon
1 teaspoon ground coriander
Mango Salsa (below)

Combine the black beans, brown rice, celery, olives, salt and pepper in a large bowl and toss. Combine the orange juice, vinegar, olive oil, orange zest, parsley, cilantro, green onions, cumin, cinnamon, coriander, salt and pepper in a jar with a tight-fitting lid. Cover and shake well. Pour over the black bean mixture and toss to coat. Serve with Mango Salsa.

Yield: 6 servings

Mango Salsa

1 orange, peeled, seeded, chopped
1 tomato, chopped
2 green onions, chopped
1/2 jalapeño, chopped
1 mango, peeled, cubed
1 tablespoon lemon or lime juice
1/4 teaspoon cumin
1/4 teaspoon coriander
1 tablespoon chopped cilantro
Salt to taste

Combine the ingredients in a bowl and toss to mix well. Chill, covered, in the refrigerator.

Yield: 6 servings

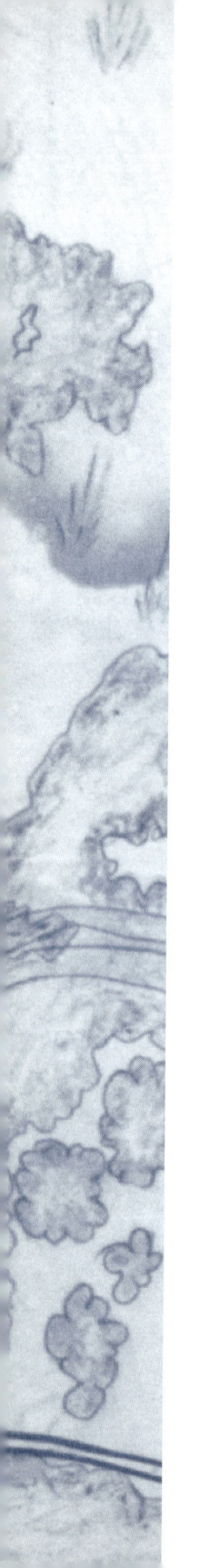

Grape Salad

1 bunch seedless green grapes
1 bunch seedless red grapes
1 cup sour cream
8 ounces cream cheese, softened
3/4 cup sugar
1 teaspoon vanilla extract

Rinse the grapes, discarding the stems and pat dry. Beat the sour cream, cream cheese, sugar and vanilla in a mixing bowl until smooth. Add the grapes and stir until coated. Chill, covered, in the refrigerator.

Yield: 6 servings

Since the establishment of Girl Scouting in Southwestern Wisconsin, Southeastern Minnesota, and Northeastern Iowa, Girl Scouts have wanted their very own camp—for many years they had camped at Spring Banks, Camp Bradfield, and Camp Decorah. After a twenty-year search, the Riverland Girl Scouts had found the perfect location—a 240-acre parcel of land near Mindoro, Wisconsin. The land was purchased using the profits from the cookie sale and soon a wave of dedicated community members, including Lillian Hope Kumm—one of the original founders of the council, would come together to create Camp Ehawee.

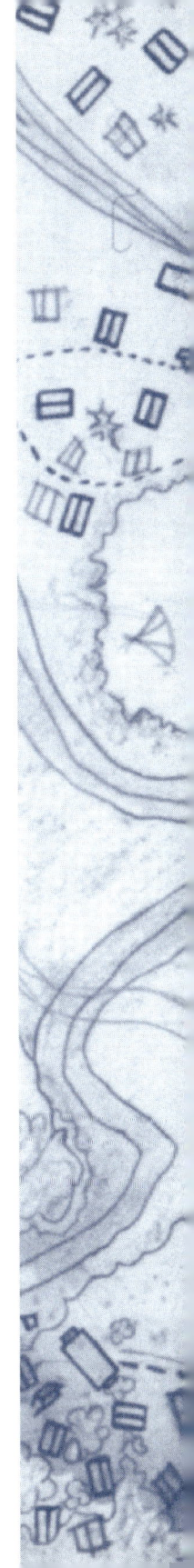

Fabulous Chicken Salad

4 chicken breasts, cooked
3 ribs celery, diagonally sliced
1 large green, red or yellow bell pepper, finely chopped
2 green onions, finely chopped
2 cups seedless red grape halves
2 cups drained canned pineapple tidbits

1 cup slivered almonds, toasted
2/3 cup mayonnaise
1/4 cup light cream or milk
2 tablespoons vinegar
1 teaspoon salt
1/8 teaspoon pepper
Lettuce leaves

Cut the chicken into large chunks, discarding the skin and bones. Combine the chicken, celery, bell pepper, green onions, grapes, pineapple and almonds in a large bowl and toss to mix. Chill, covered, in the refrigerator.

Blend the mayonnaise, cream, vinegar, salt and pepper in a bowl. Chill, covered, in the refrigerator. Just before serving, add the mayonnaise mixture to the chicken mixture and toss lightly. Serve on lettuce-lined salad plates.

Yield: 8 to 10 servings

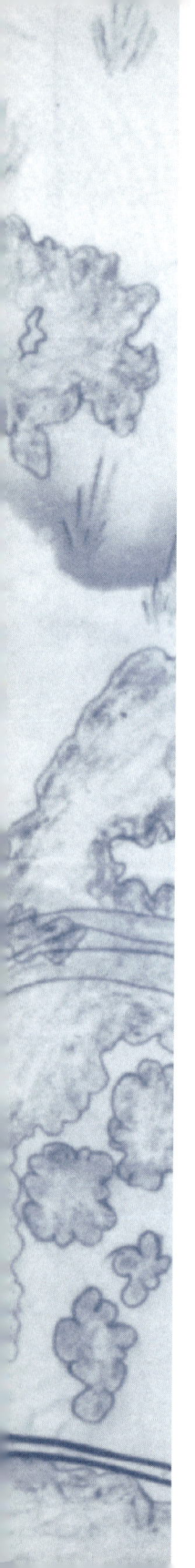

Oriental Chicken Salad

1/2 cup sugar
1 tablespoon cornstarch
1/4 cup water
1/4 cup vegetable oil
1/4 cup ketchup
3 tablespoons cider vinegar
1 tablespoon soy sauce
1 medium head iceberg lettuce, torn
2 cups chopped cooked chicken
1 cup salted cashews
1 (8-ounce) can sliced water chestnuts, drained
1 (6-ounce) package frozen snow peas, thawed
1/4 cup chopped green onions
1 (3-ounce) can chow mein noodles

Bring the sugar, cornstarch, water, oil, ketchup, vinegar and soy sauce to a boil in a small saucepan. Cook for 2 minutes or until thickened, stirring constantly. Remove from the heat and cool.

Combine the lettuce, chicken, cashews, water chestnuts, snow peas, green onions and chow mein noodles in a large salad bowl and toss to mix. Add the dressing and toss to coat. Serve immediately.

Yield: 8 to 10 servings

Taco Salad

1 pound ground beef
1 (16-ounce) can kidney beans, drained
1 cup French or western salad dressing
1/2 cup taco sauce
2 to 4 tomatoes, cut into wedges
1 cup shredded sharp Cheddar cheese
1 onion, thinly sliced, separated into rings
1 head lettuce, chopped
2 cups crushed tortilla chips

Brown the ground beef in a skillet, stirring until crumbly; drain. Combine the ground beef, kidney beans, salad dressing and taco sauce in a bowl and mix well. Chill, covered, for 30 minutes. Add the tomatoes, cheese, onion and lettuce and toss to mix. Add the tortilla chips just before serving and toss to mix.

Yield: 12 servings

Each Girl Scout values the principle that she is a sister to every Girl Scout. To forge a relationship with their distant "sister," local Girl Scouts created Friendship Bags and gave them as gifts to the Girl Guides of Norway and Holland who had lost so much during World War II. They also voluntarily gave to the Juliette Low Friendship Fund, which benefits both Girl Scouts and Girl Guides abroad.

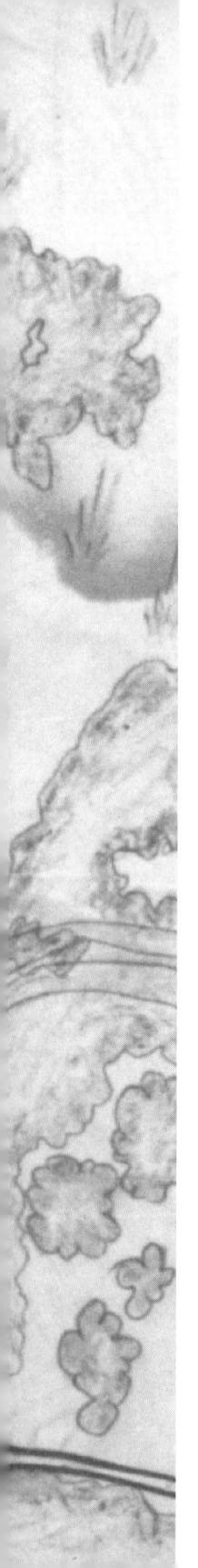

Wild Rice Chick-Pea Shrimp Salad

2/3 cup uncooked wild rice
1 teaspoon thyme
12 ounces large shrimp, cooked, peeled, deveined
1 sweet red onion, thinly sliced
1 (6-ounce) can sliced black olives, drained

1 (16-ounce) can chick-peas or garbanzo beans
1 (2-ounce) jar sliced pimento, drained
Lettuce leaves
Lemon Vinaigrette (below)

Cook the wild rice using the package directions, adding the thyme to the water. Let stand until cool. Combine the cooled wild rice, shrimp, red onion, black olives, chick-peas and pimento in a large bowl and toss to mix. Spoon into a lettuce-lined salad bowl. Drizzle with Lemon Vinaigrette.

Yield: 8 servings

Lemon Vinaigrette

1/4 cup lemon juice
1 tablespoon Dijon mustard
1 teaspoon dillweed

1 teaspoon chervil
1/3 cup olive oil or safflower oil
Salt and pepper to taste

Combine the lemon juice, Dijon mustard, dillweed and chervil in a small bowl and whisk well. Add the olive oil and whisk well to blend. Season with salt and pepper.

Yield: 2/3 cup

Glazed Carrots with Dill

3 large carrots, sliced
3/4 cup chicken broth
1 tablespoon brown sugar
1/2 teaspoon dried dill
1/2 teaspoon white pepper
1/2 teaspoon lemon juice

Combine the carrots, chicken broth, brown sugar, dill and white pepper in a small saucepan. Bring to a boil. Cook for 8 minutes or until the carrots are tender and the liquid evaporates. Stir in the lemon juice.

Yield: 4 servings

Following in the tradition of the first Girl Scout Handbook, "How Girls Can Help Their Country," regional Girl Scouts donated both time and service during our country's greatest time of need. During World War II, local Girl Scouts responded to the United Nations call by collecting rags, paper, and metal—some Girl Scouts organized to create troop Victory Gardens to raise and preserve thousands of pounds of vegetables for servicemen overseas.

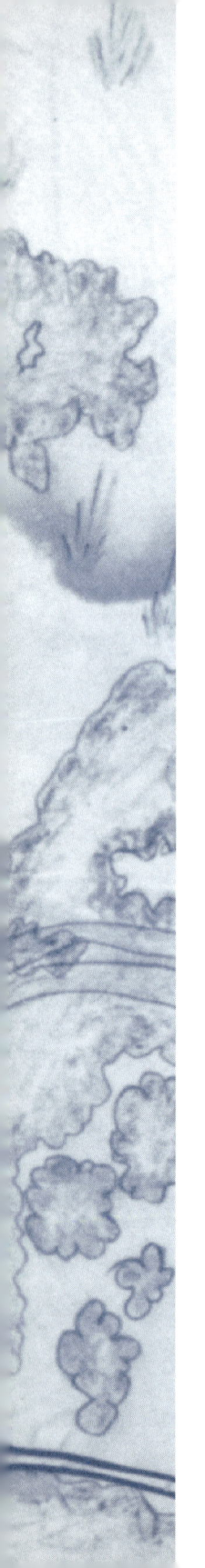

Potatoes Elegante

6 medium potatoes, peeled, thinly sliced
1/3 cup butter, melted
1 cup grated Parmesan cheese

Rinse the potatoes and pat dry. Brush 1 tablespoon of the butter on the bottom and side of a 9-inch pie plate. Sprinkle with 1 tablespoon of the Parmesan cheese. Toss the potatoes with the remaining butter in a bowl.

Layer the potatoes and remaining Parmesan cheese 1/2 at a time in the prepared pie plate. Bake at 400 degrees for 1 hour or until the potatoes are tender. Invert immediately onto a serving plate.

Yield: 4 to 6 servings

What does "Ehawee" mean? Thanks to Jacqueline Kramer from Troop 27 in La Crosse, the new camp was named Camp Ehawee for the HoChunk Indian phrase meaning "Laughing Maidens." Today, fifty years later, Camp Ehawee has expanded to offer 308 acres of activity and serves over 1000 children.

Pineapple-Glazed Yams

4 large yams
Salt to taste
1/4 cup (1/2 stick) butter
1/2 cup packed brown sugar or honey
1 teaspoon salt
1 teaspoon grated orange zest
1 cup undrained crushed pineapple
2 teaspoons cornstarch
2 tablespoons water

Peel the yams. Cut into thick slices. Boil in salted water in a saucepan for 10 minutes or until tender. Melt the butter in a large skillet. Stir in the brown sugar, 1 teaspoon salt, orange zest and pineapple.

Dissolve the cornstarch in the water in a small bowl. Stir into the pineapple mixture. Cook until thickened, stirring constantly. Turn off the heat. Drain the yams. Alternate layers of the yams and pineapple mixture in a buttered dish until all ingredients are used. Serve immediately.

Yield: 6 to 8 servings

Note: You may prepare this recipe ahead of time and refrigerate. Reheat in the microwave or oven before serving.

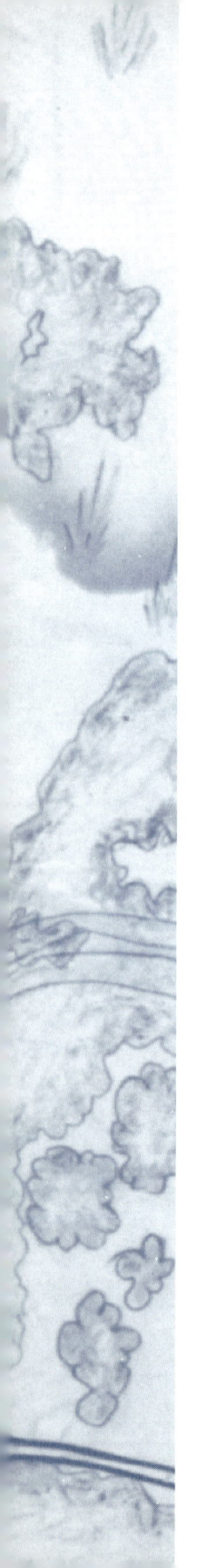

Two-Grain Vegetable Casserole

2 medium carrots
1 cup fresh mushroom quarters
1 cup rinsed drained canned black beans
1 cup whole kernel corn
1 cup vegetable broth

1/2 cup pearl barley
1/4 cup bulgur
1/3 cup chopped fresh parsley
1/4 cup chopped onion
1/4 teaspoon garlic powder
1/2 cup shredded Cheddar cheese

Cut the carrots into halves lengthwise. Cut into thin slices. Combine the carrots, mushrooms, black beans, corn, vegetable broth, barley, bulgur, parsley, onion and garlic powder in a large bowl and mix well. Spoon into a 1 1/2-quart baking dish.

Bake, covered, at 350 degrees for 1 hour, stirring once halfway through the baking time. Sprinkle with the cheese. Cover and let stand for 5 minutes or until the cheese melts.

Yield: 6 servings

As Camp Ehawee began to flourish, so did the World Girl Scout Organization. In 1953, two million girls called Girl Scouting their organization. The list of girls who wished to join Girl Scouting grew and each leader accepted the responsibility of adding new girls to her troop. By 1957, three million Girl Scouts called Girl Scouting their organization.

Mushroom Strudel

3 cups chopped mushrooms
1 Vidalia onion, julienned
1/8 teaspoon minced garlic
1 tablespoon olive oil
1 teaspoon Worcestershire sauce
1 cup crumbled bleu cheese
1 (8-count) can crescent rolls
3 ounces cream cheese, softened
1/4 cup grated Parmesan cheese

Sauté the mushrooms, onion and garlic in the olive oil in a skillet. Add the Worcestershire sauce and mix well. Remove from the heat to cool. Stir in the bleu cheese. Unroll the crescent roll dough.

Line an ungreased 8-inch round baking pan with the dough, pressing the perforations to seal. Spread the cream cheese over the dough. Layer the mushroom mixture over the cream cheese. Sprinkle with the Parmesan cheese. Bake at 350 degrees for 20 to 25 minutes or until cooked through.

Yield: 4 to 6 servings

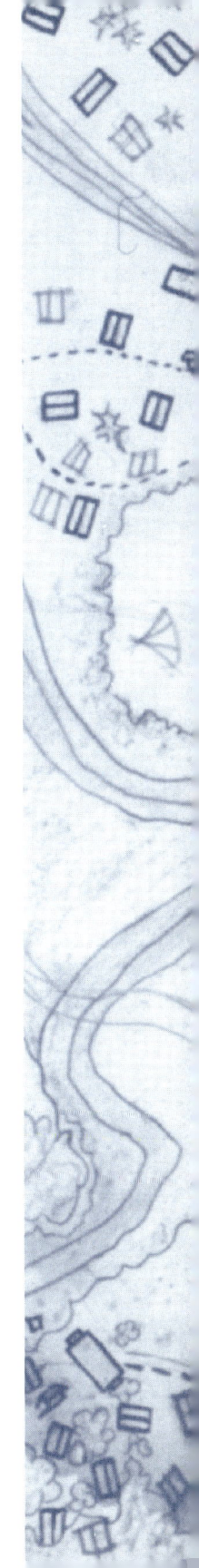

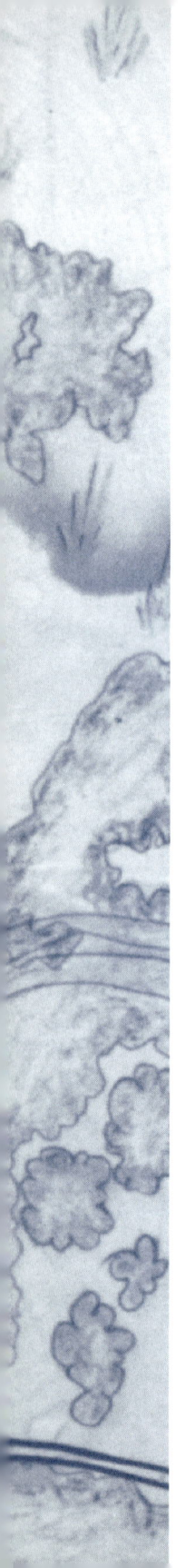

Apple Raisin Wild Rice Pilaf

1 cup wild rice
3 cups apple cider
1 1/2 cups water
6 tablespoons margarine
1/2 cup slivered almonds

1/2 cup raisins
1 large apple, peeled, chopped
1/2 teaspoon pepper
1/2 teaspoon cinnamon
1/4 teaspoon nutmeg

Rinse the wild rice in hot water; drain. Combine the wild rice, apple cider and 1 1/2 cups water in a large saucepan. Bring to a boil and reduce the heat. Stir the rice mixture and cover. Simmer for 40 to 45 minutes or until the wild rice is cooked through; drain.

Melt the margarine in a heavy skillet. Add the almonds and raisins. Sauté over medium heat until the almonds are toasted. Add the apple, pepper, cinnamon and nutmeg. Sauté for 2 minutes. Stir in the wild rice. Cook until heated through.

Yield: 6 servings

Of vegetables I should like to say they can scarcely be too much cooked. Wash well in salted water; let leafy ones have a swim to get rid of grasshoppers and caterpillars and sand, then put them into boiling salted water, and take off the lid.

Excerpt from "How Girls Can Help Their Country,"
The 1913 "Handbook for Girl Scouts" by W. J. Hoxie

Spiced Rice with Almonds

3 tablespoons slivered almonds
2 tablespoons vegetable oil
1 medium onion, thinly sliced
1 garlic clove, minced
1 cup uncooked long-grain rice
1/4 teaspoon cardamom
1/8 teaspoon ginger
Dash of ground red pepper, cinnamon, cumin and nutmeg
1 3/4 cups chicken broth

Sauté the almonds in the hot oil in a medium saucepan until light brown. Remove to paper towels to drain. Add the onion and garlic to the saucepan. Sauté until the onion is tender but not brown. Add the uncooked rice, cardamom, ginger, red pepper, cinnamon, cumin and nutmeg and mix well.

Sauté for 3 minutes or until the rice is brown. Add the chicken broth. Bring to a boil and reduce the heat. Simmer, covered, for 15 minutes. Remove from the heat. Let stand, covered, for 10 minutes. Stir in the sautéed almonds. Serve immediately.

Yield: 4 to 6 servings

OSSE COUNTY　　　　　　　　　　　SACAJAWEA

RIVER

MINNEHAHA

DINNING LODGE

PARKING LOT

POOL

MARINUKA

COOK OUT　　COOK OUT

Regional Fare

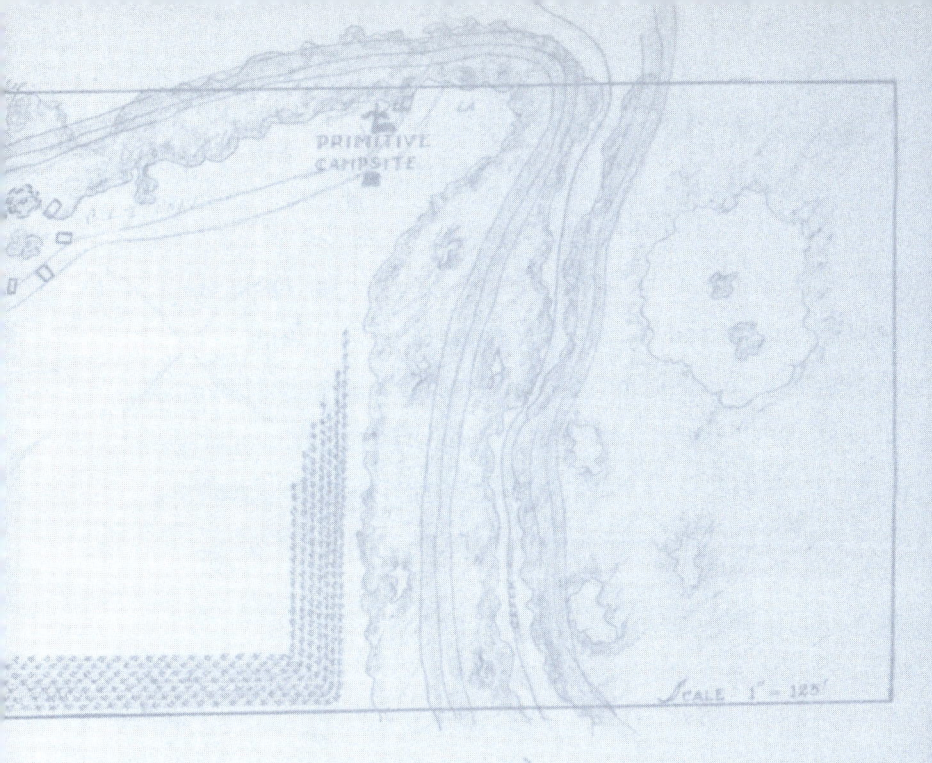

Recipes from the Upper Mississippi Valley

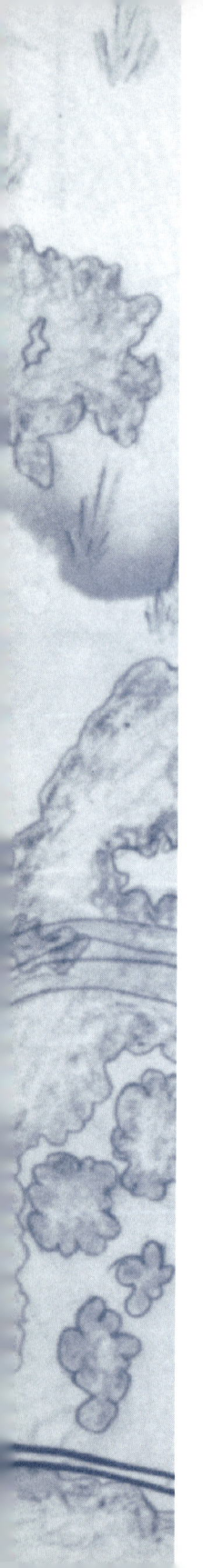

Field's Famous Chicken Potpie

The very first restaurant at Field's began in 1890 when Mrs. Hering, an employee in our millinery department, served her lunch, homemade chicken potpies, to hungry ladies shopping in her department. So successful, it impressed upon Marshall Field the need for a respectable place downtown to eat. When the first tearoom opened in April of 1890, not only did it attract thousands daily, but it would become the first formal dining room inside any retail store.

> 2 tablespoons plus 1 teaspoon chicken fat or butter
> 3 tablespoons all-purpose flour
> 1 1/2 cups chicken broth
> 3/4 teaspoon salt (optional)
> 6 ounces green peas
> 6 ounces (3/8-inch) chopped carrots
> 12 ounces chopped cooked chicken breasts
> 6 unbaked (4-inch) pie shells
> 6 unbaked (4-inch) pie pastries

Combine the chicken fat and flour in a small saucepan. Cook over low heat until thickened and smooth, stirring constantly. Heat the chicken broth in a small saucepan. Add to the flour mixture and beat vigorously with a wire whisk.

Cook over low heat for 5 minutes or until smooth, stirring constantly. Season with salt. Add the peas and carrots. Stir in the chicken. Spoon equal amounts of the chicken mixture into each pie shell. Top each with a pie pastry, trimming and fluting the edge. Bake at 400 degrees for 23 to 30 minutes or until golden brown.

Yield: 6 servings

Some History Behind Marshall Field's

The start of a new millennium seems a most appropriate time to celebrate the uniting of three great department stores under one great name. In 2001, Dayton's and Hudson's joined under the Marshall Field's banner to create a bigger, better shopping experience for the guests we've been proud to serve throughout the twentieth century.

From its beginnings in downtown Chicago in 1852, Marshall Field's has earned a reputation of excellence through its landmark achievements, making it one of the premier department stores in the United States. Always a leader and innovator, Marshall Field's was the first department store to establish a European buying office in Manchester, England. It was the first to open a dining room restaurant and the first to offer a bridal registry. In addition, the store has established many lines of exclusive private-label merchandise, including our world-famous Frango® chocolates, and departments that are devoted to exquisite antique furniture, silver, and jewelry.

The Marshall Field's family of stores has a rich history of contributing 5 percent of its federally taxable income to community nonprofit organizations, including support for the arts through our Project Imagine initiative.

Chicken Tenderloins with Cranberry Mustard Sauce

1 pound chicken tenderloins
All-purpose flour for coating
Salt and pepper to taste
2 tablespoons butter
2 tablespoons vegetable oil
2/3 cup dry white wine
2/3 cup chicken broth

3 tablespoons Dijon mustard
1 1/2 teaspoons cornstarch
1 1/2 tablespoons water
1/2 cup Craisins (dried cranberries)
1/4 cup sliced green onion tops

Toss the chicken in flour in a shallow dish to coat lightly. Shake off the excess flour and sprinkle lightly with salt and pepper. Heat 1/2 of the butter and 1/2 of the oil in a large skillet. Add 1/2 of the chicken.

Cook for 2 minutes or until cooked through and golden brown, turning once. Remove to a warm platter and keep warm. Repeat the process with the remaining butter, oil and chicken.

Add the wine, chicken broth and Dijon mustard to the skillet, stirring constantly to deglaze the skillet. Mix the cornstarch and water in a bowl. Add to the skillet. Stir in the Craisins. Boil for 1 to 2 minutes or until thickened, stirring constantly. Stir in the green onions. Cook for 1 minute. Pour over the chicken.

Yield: 4 servings

Note: This recipe provided courtesy of Ocean Spray.

Cranberried Chicken

1 (3-pound) chicken, cut up
1 (16-ounce) can whole cranberry sauce
1 envelope onion soup mix
1 (8-ounce) bottle Russian salad dressing

Arrange the chicken in a baking dish. Mix the cranberry sauce, soup mix and salad dressing in a bowl. Pour over the chicken. Marinate, covered, in the refrigerator for 24 hours. Bake, uncovered, at 325 degrees for 1 1/2 hours or until the chicken is cooked through, spooning the glaze over the chicken twice. Serve with rice or your favorite potato dish.

Yield: 4 to 6 servings

Note: This recipe provided courtesy of Ocean Spray.

Grilled River Duck Breasts

2 large duck breasts
1/2 teaspoon paprika
1 tablespoon butter, melted
1 tablespoon lemon juice
1 teaspoon grated lemon zest
1 teaspoon Worcestershire sauce
1 tablespoon ketchup

Sprinkle the duck with the paprika. Place in a sealable plastic food storage bag. Mix the butter, lemon juice, lemon zest, Worcestershire sauce and ketchup in a small bowl. Pour over the duck and seal the bag. Marinate at room temperature for 1 hour. Drain the duck, reserving the marinade. Bring the reserved marinade to a boil in a small saucepan. Boil for 2 minutes, stirring constantly. Remove from the heat. Arrange the duck on a grill rack. Grill for 12 minutes or until golden brown, basting frequently with the cooked reserved marinade. Cover the grill and reduce the heat if possible. Grill for 20 minutes longer.

Yield: 2 or 3 servings

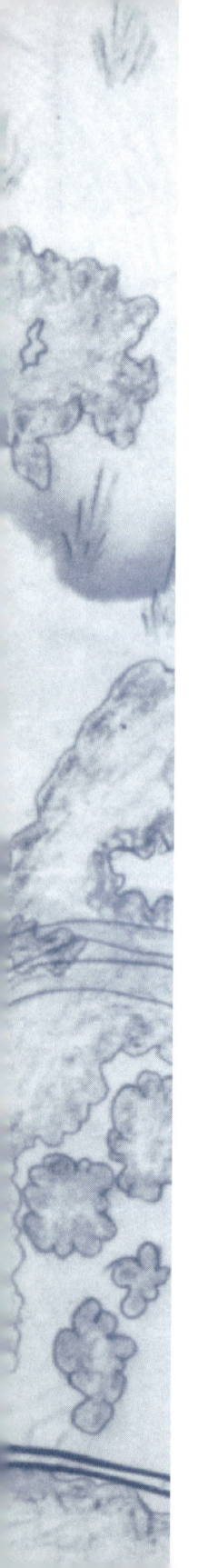

Sweet River Duck

4 ducks, quartered
1/2 cup apricot preserves
1/2 cup lemon juice
Grated zest of 1 lemon
1/2 teaspoon ginger
1 lemon, sliced

Arrange the ducks in a baking dish. Spread with the apricot preserves. Pour the lemon juice over the ducks. Sprinkle with the lemon zest.

Marinate, covered, in the refrigerator for 6 to 12 hours, turning twice. Sprinkle with the ginger. Top with the lemon slices. Bake, uncovered, at 350 degrees for 1 to 1 1/2 hours or until the juices run clear.

Yield: 6 to 8 servings

As the Golden Anniversary arrived for Girl Scouting, Riverland Council was prospering from both a successful program and a strong community. The 1960s showed the success of the Camp, which many dedicated volunteers had created. The late Elenora Gund wanted to see this program continue past her time, so she generously donated the funds to "burn the mortgage" for Camp Ehawee—ensuring that Girl Scouts of Riverland would always have a camp to call home.

Cranberry-Stuffed Pork Chops

6 rib pork chops with pockets, 1 1/2 inches thick
1/2 cup finely chopped celery
1/2 cup finely chopped onion
1/2 cup fresh Wisconsin cranberries
2 tablespoons butter
1 cup seasoned bread crumbs
1/4 cup sugar
1/2 teaspoon salt
1/8 teaspoon pepper
1/4 teaspoon poultry seasoning

Brown the pork chops on each side in a hot nonstick skillet. Sauté the celery, onion and cranberries in the butter in a skillet. Combine the bread crumbs, sugar, salt, pepper and poultry seasoning in a bowl and mix well. Add to the cranberry mixture and mix well.

Stuff into the pork chops. Arrange in a baking dish. Bake at 350 degrees for 1 hour or until a meat thermometer registers 170 degrees when inserted into the thickest portion.

Yield: 6 servings

Note: This recipe provided courtesy of Ocean Spray.

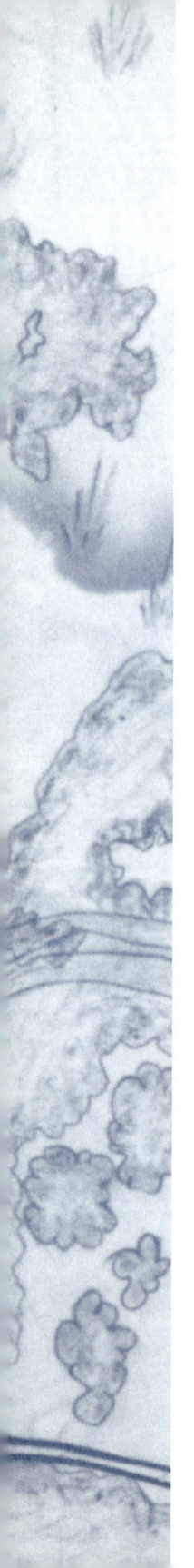

Crispy Catfish

3/4 cup finely crushed saltines (about 22 crackers)
1 teaspoon seasoned salt
1/2 teaspoon celery salt
1/2 teaspoon garlic salt
4 (8-ounce) catfish fillets
1/3 cup butter or margarine, melted

Combine the saltines, seasoned salt, celery salt and garlic salt in a shallow dish and mix well. Pat the fish dry. Dip in the butter and coat with the crumb mixture. Coat a skillet with nonstick cooking spray. Add the fish. Fry, covered, over medium heat for 10 minutes or until the fish flakes easily with a fork, carefully turning once.

Yield: 4 servings

The week of March 12th always marks the birthday for Girl Scouting in the United States. In 1967, Riverland Council celebrated its 50th anniversary. To demonstrate the effect Girl Scouting had on his community, Mayor Victor Ellefson proclaimed Girl Scouting—"A Promise in Action." Girl Scouting inspires girls with the highest ideals of character, conduct, patriotism, and service so that they may become resourceful citizens.

Spicy Catfish

2 pounds catfish fillets
1/4 cup tomato paste
1 tomato, peeled, chopped
1 cup Italian salad dressing
1/4 teaspoon red pepper flakes
3 tablespoons chopped fresh parsley
3 tablespoons grated Romano cheese

Cut the fish into serving-size portions and pat dry. Arrange the fish in a well-greased baking dish. Combine the tomato paste, tomato, salad dressing, red pepper flakes and parsley in a bowl and mix well. Pour over the fish, coating well.

Sprinkle with the Romano cheese. Bake at 350 degrees for 20 to 25 minutes or until the fish flakes easily. Broil 3 inches from the heat source for 2 to 3 minutes or until crisp and bubbly.

Yield: 6 servings

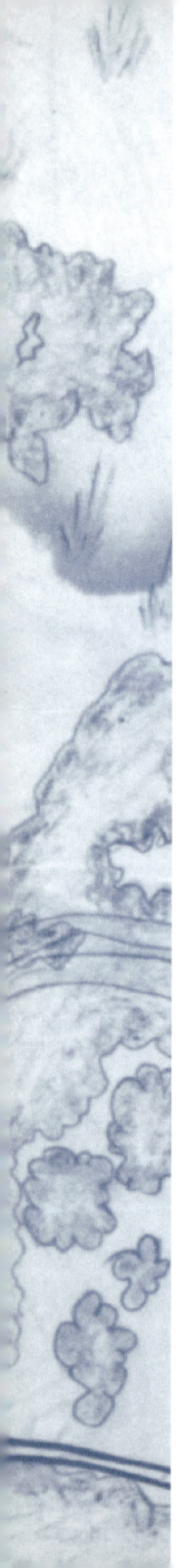

Limey Muskie (Muskellunge)

1 muskellunge (pike), cut into 1-inch-thick steaks
1 cup lime juice
Grated zest of 2 limes
1 cup all-purpose flour
2 tablespoons butter
1/3 cup corn oil

Arrange the fish in a shallow dish. Pour the lime juice over the fish. Sprinkle with the lime zest. Marinate, covered, in the refrigerator for 2 to 3 hours. Drain the fish, discarding the marinade. Dredge the fish in the flour. Heat the butter and corn oil in a skillet. Add the fish. Fry until the fish flakes easily and is golden brown on both sides. Drain on paper towels. Serve hot.

Yield: 6 to 8 servings

As women began to work outside their homes following the World War II years, Girl Scouting began to shift its focus. Expanding on the existing foundation of housekeeping and community service, Girl Scouts began adding career exploration components into existing badges, helping to provide more opportunity for those girls who wished to pursue one of the many new careers being offered to women.

Stuffed Brook Trout

4 to 6 whole trout, cleaned
1 cup cooked brown rice
1 cup chopped celery
1 cup sliced mushrooms
1/2 onion, chopped
1 (2-ounce) jar chopped pimentos, drained
1/2 cup nonfat yogurt or sour cream
1 (10-ounce) can cream of mushroom soup
1 lemon, sliced

Arrange each whole fish on a double layer of heavy-duty foil. Combine the brown rice, celery, mushrooms, onion, pimentos, yogurt and soup in a bowl and mix well. Stuff into the fish cavities. Top each fish with the lemon slices. Fold the foil to enclose each fish securely.

Place on a grill rack. Grill over medium heat for 20 to 25 minutes or until the fish flakes easily.

Yield: 4 to 6 servings

Settler's Venison

1 (4- to 6-pound) venison roast
1 cup maple syrup

Place the venison in a sealable plastic food storage bag. Pour the maple syrup over the venison and seal the bag. Marinate in the refrigerator for 2 days, turning at least twice each day. Arrange the venison on a rack in a roasting pan. Bake at 275 degrees for 3 hours or until tender.

Yield: 4 to 6 servings

Venison Steaks

4 to 6 venison steaks
1/2 cup vegetable or olive oil
1 cup red wine
1 onion, chopped
1/4 cup Dijon mustard
1/2 teaspoon oregano
1/4 teaspoon basil
2 garlic cloves, crushed

Arrange the venison in a shallow dish. Process the oil, red wine, onion, Dijon mustard, oregano, basil and garlic in a blender or food processor until blended. Pour over the venison. Marinate, covered, in the refrigerator for 24 hours, turning twice. Arrange the venison on a grill rack. Grill until the venison is of the desired degree of doneness.

Yield: 4 to 6 servings

Note: You may also broil the venison on a rack in a broiler pan.

How to Deal with Fires and Accidents

Fire—If you discover a house on fire you should—
  1st—Alarm the people inside.
  2nd—Warn the nearest policeman or fire-brigade station.
  3rd—Rouse neighbours to bring ladders, mattresses, carpets, to catch people jumping.

After arrival of fire engines the best thing Guides can do is to help the police in keeping back the crowd out of the way of the firemen, hose, etc.

There is a useful kind of drill called "Scrum" for keeping back the crowd. The Guides form a line, or double line, and pass their arms around each other's waists, and shove, head down, into the crowd, and so drive it back.

Moving an Insensible Girl

Excerpt from "Girl Guiding" by Lord Baden-Powell, 1938

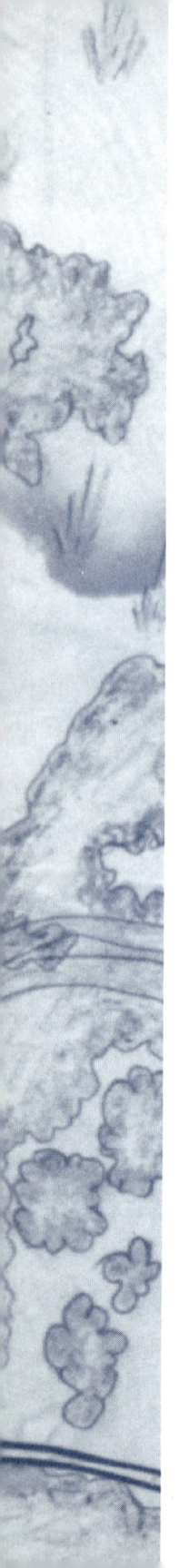

Venison Fingers

1/2 cup olive oil
1/4 cup red wine vinegar
1 teaspoon oregano
1 teaspoon basil

1 garlic clove, crushed
1 1/2 to 2 pounds venison steaks
2 cups unseasoned cracker meal
1/2 cup olive oil

Combine 1/2 cup olive oil, red wine vinegar, oregano, basil and garlic in a bowl and mix well. Cut the venison into finger-size strips and place in a sealable plastic food storage bag. Add the marinade and seal the bag.

Marinate in the refrigerator for 12 to 24 hours. Drain the venison slightly, discarding the marinade. Dredge the venison in the cracker meal, patting firmly to coat. Heat 1/2 cup olive oil to 325 degrees in an electric skillet. Add the venison. Sauté until golden brown. Drain on paper towels. Serve hot.

Yield: 6 servings

"Girl Scouting—A Tradition with a Future" best explains what each supporter of Girl Scouting already knows. Girl Scouting teaches young women how to reach for their dreams. In a joint effort with the Gateway Area Boy Scouts, Riverland Council went out and campaigned for the character of youth. Together they raised funds to improve both the Camp Ehawee and Camp Decorah programs. Today, thousands benefit from the vast offerings of each camp thanks to the volunteers and donors who constantly work to keep the tradition of success going.

Venison Stroganoff

1/2 cup all-purpose flour
1/2 teaspoon salt
1/2 teaspoon pepper
2 pounds venison, cubed
1/4 cup olive oil or canola oil
4 medium onions, chopped
2 cups beef or venison broth
1/4 cup red wine (optional)
8 ounces fresh mushrooms, sliced
1 (10-ounce) can cream of mushroom soup
1 1/2 cups nonfat sour cream

Mix the flour, salt and pepper in a sealable plastic food storage bag. Add the venison and shake to coat. Brown the venison mixture in the olive oil in an electric skillet set at medium-high. Add the onions, broth, wine, mushrooms and soup and stir to mix well.

Reduce the heat setting to low. Simmer, covered, for 2 to 3 hours, stirring occasionally. Stir in the sour cream. Simmer for 30 minutes, stirring occasionally. Serve over noodles or rice.

Yield: 6 to 8 servings

After-Church Venison Stew

1 1/2 pounds venison or lean beef, cut into 1 1/2-inch cubes
2 teaspoons salt
1/4 teaspoon pepper
1/2 teaspoon basil
2 ribs celery, cut diagonally into slices
4 medium carrots, quartered
2 medium onions, cut into 1/2-inch slices
1 (10-ounce) can tomato soup
1/2 soup can water
3 medium potatoes, peeled, cut into cubes

Arrange the venison in a 3-quart baking dish. Sprinkle with the salt, pepper and basil. Layer the celery, carrots and onions over the venison. Mix the soup and water in a small bowl. Pour over the top, coating all pieces. Bake, tightly covered, at 300 degrees for 3 hours. Add the potatoes. Bake for 1 hour longer.

Yield: 5 servings

Note: You may thicken the pan juices with a small amount of flour if desired. You may prepare in a slow cooker by bringing to a boil on High and then reducing to Low.

Today Girl Scouts have much to be thankful for. Many have learned to be stronger, have become comfortable challenging themselves, and have become who they are thanks to the volunteers, staff, dedicated community supporters, and visionaries of Girl Scouting. Whether the program has changed to open doors to new things or held steadfast to the principles of acceptance and service, Girl Scouts everywhere know that someone is looking out for them. We thank all of you who have helped Girls Grow Strong! Thank you!!

Morels in Puff Pastry

4 puff pastry shells
6 green onions
1 tablespoon butter
1 tablespoon olive oil
1/2 teaspoon cumin
1/2 teaspoon fines herbes or other gourmet blend
2 cups sliced morel mushrooms
1 cup sliced shiitake mushrooms
2 tablespoons medium sherry
Salt and pepper to taste
Chopped fresh parsley to taste

Bake the puff pastry shells using the package directions. Cut the green onions diagonally into slices, keeping the white and green parts separated. Melt the butter in the olive oil in a skillet over low heat. Add the white part of the green onions. Sauté until tender; do not brown.

Sprinkle with the cumin and fines herbes. Add the mushrooms. Cook, covered, over low heat for 10 minutes or until the mushrooms soften. Add the sherry. Cook, uncovered, for 5 minutes. Season with salt and pepper. Stir in the green onion tops. Cook for 1 minute. Turn off the heat. Spoon the mushroom mixture into the baked pastry shells. Sprinkle with chopped parsley.

Yield: 4 servings

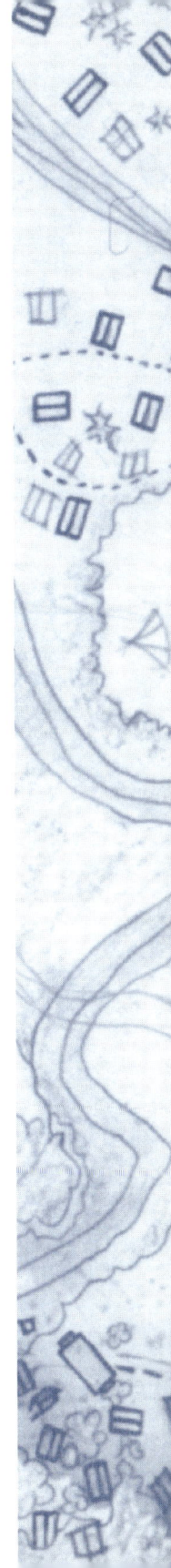

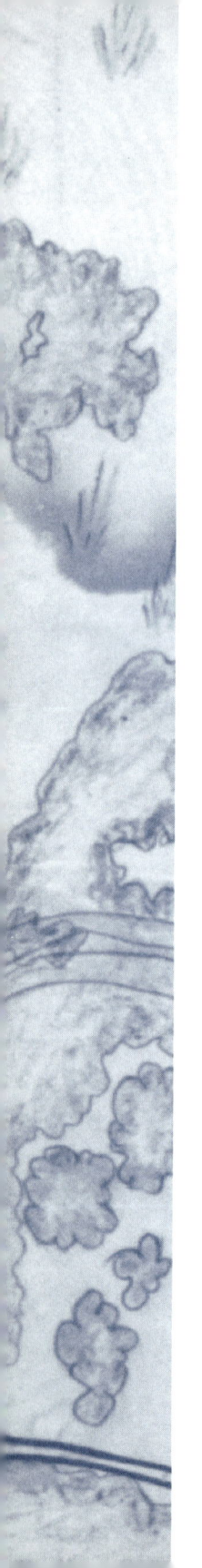

Wilted Dandelions

3 cups dandelion greens
6 slices bacon, chopped
⅓ cup white wine vinegar
Salt and pepper to taste

Rinse the dandelion greens; drain. Tear into bite-size pieces. Fry the bacon in a skillet until crisp. Remove the bacon with a slotted spoon to paper towels to drain. Crumble the bacon. Add the white wine vinegar to the bacon drippings in the skillet. Bring to a boil, stirring to deglaze the skillet. Add the dandelion greens and toss until wilted and heated through. Season with salt and pepper. Sprinkle with the crumbled bacon. Serve immediately.

Yield: 4 servings

Note: If you pick your own dandelion greens, pick only the very young leaves growing in shaded areas and make sure they are herbicide free. The lighter the color, the better the taste.

Pumpkin Wild Rice Soup

1 cup chopped onion
2 tablespoons butter
4 cups chicken broth
1 (16-ounce) can pumpkin
1⅓ cups cooked wild rice
⅛ teaspoon white pepper
1 cup heavy cream
Chopped fresh chives to taste

Sauté the onion in the butter in a large saucepan. Stir in the broth and pumpkin. Cook over low heat for 10 to 15 minutes, stirring occasionally. Stir in the wild rice and white pepper. Cook for 10 minutes. Stir in the heavy cream. Cook until heated through; do not boil. Sprinkle with chives. Ladle into soup bowls. Serve immediately.

Yield: 8 servings

Five Thousand Pine Trees

My mother, Marge Spildie, showed me the letter she received from the Girl Scouts. She's 82 years old now and was a Girl Scout in 1931. Our family has been in Girl Scouts since then. I was a Girl Scout in the early 1950s, my sister followed, then my two daughters and now my granddaughters. We still have all of our badges.

The camp was new then, only tents and not even a name. My troop entered the contest to name it. My friend, Jackie Kramer, won the contest and Camp Ehawee was born.

The memory my mom and dad shared was when dad (Ellerd Spildie) went to camp to help plant 5000 pine trees. He's passed on now, but the trees will live on forever.

What a great place to camp. Our troop really was full of "laughing maidens"!

Kay Wright, Onalaska, Wisconsin

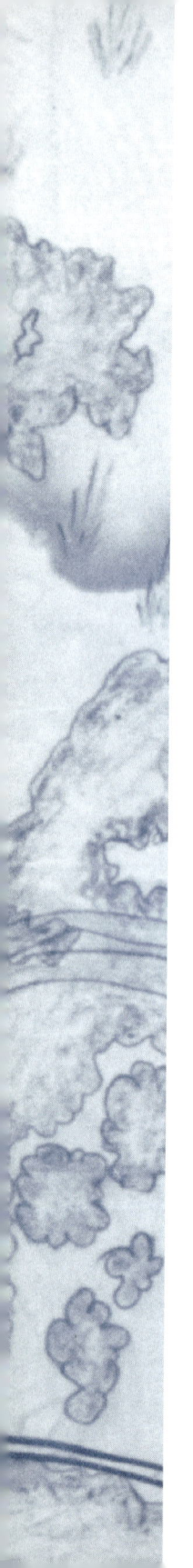

German Vegetable Soup

2 cups chicken broth
1/4 cup tomato purée
1 bay leaf
1/2 teaspoon sugar
Dash of pepper
1 large carrot, chopped

1 cup chopped rutabaga
1 cup chopped potato
1/4 cup sugar snap peas
1 small onion, chopped
8 ounces kielbasa, sliced
1 cup chopped cabbage

Combine the chicken broth, tomato purée, bay leaf, sugar and pepper in a large saucepan. Add the carrot, rutabaga, potato, snap peas, onion and kielbasa. Bring to a boil and reduce the heat. Simmer for 30 to 40 minutes. Add the cabbage. Cook until the cabbage is tender. Discard the bay leaf. Ladle into soup bowls. Serve immediately.

Yield: 4 to 6 servings

"Come right over! I've got something for the girls of Savannah and America... and we are going to start it tonight!" is the famous quotation that began it all. On this night, March 12, 1912, Juliette Gordon Low founded what would become the largest organization for girls in the world—the Girl Scouts of America. Since its creation, it has touched the lives of millions of girls and adults the world over.

Wisconsin Chicken Vegetable Soup

3/4 cup chopped onion
1/2 tablespoon butter
1/2 cup chopped carrot
1/2 cup chopped celery
1/2 cup chopped sweet potato
1/2 cup chopped russet potato
1/2 cup whole kernel corn
1/2 cup sliced mushrooms

1/2 cup chopped tomato
1/2 cup chopped zucchini
6 cups chicken broth
1/2 teaspoon Italian seasoning
1/4 teaspoon pepper
2 chicken breasts, cooked, chopped
1 tablespoon chopped parsley

Sauté the onion in the butter in a medium saucepan for 2 minutes or until tender. Add the carrot, celery, sweet potato and russet potato. Cook for 3 minutes. Add the corn, mushrooms, tomato and zucchini. Cook for 3 minutes.

Add the chicken broth, Italian seasoning, pepper and chicken. Bring to a boil and reduce the heat. Simmer for 10 minutes.

Ladle into soup bowls. Sprinkle with the parsley. Serve with your favorite crusty bread.

Yield: 10 servings

LA CROSSE COUNTY　　　　　　　　　SACAJAWEA

RIVER

MINNEHAHA

DINNING LODGE

PARKING LOT

POOL

MARINUKA

COOK OUT　　　COOK OUT

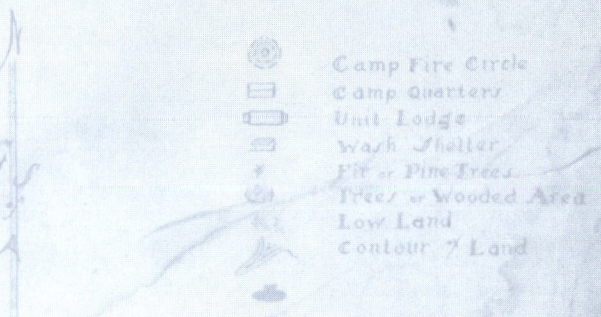

Rush Hour Cooking
Recipes in Thirty Minutes or Less

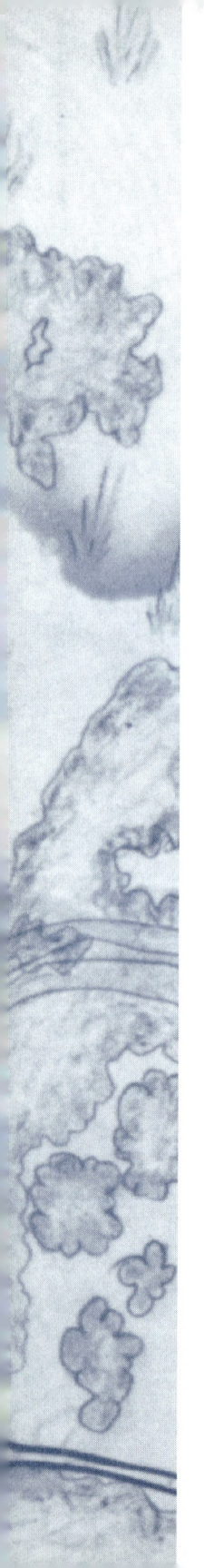

Country Chicken Chowder

1 pound chicken tenders
2 tablespoons butter or margarine
1 small carrot, sliced
1 (10-ounce) can cream of potato soup
1 cup milk
1 cup frozen whole kernel corn
Salt and pepper to taste

Cut the chicken into 1/2-inch pieces. Melt the butter in a large saucepan over medium heat. Add the chicken. Sauté for 10 minutes. Add the carrot.

Sauté for 3 minutes. Stir in the soup, milk and corn. Cook over low heat for 10 minutes or until the corn is tender and the chowder is heated thorough. Season with salt and pepper. Ladle into soup bowls. Serve immediately.

Yield: 4 servings

Lunch Box Pizzas

1 (10-count) can buttermilk biscuits
1/4 cup tomato sauce
1 teaspoon Italian seasoning
10 slices pepperoni
3/4 cup shredded mozzarella cheese

Unroll the biscuit dough and separate into 10 portions. Roll each portion into a 3-inch circle. Press each circle into a greased muffin cup. Mix the tomato sauce and Italian seasoning in a bowl. Spoon 1 teaspoonful into each prepared cup. Top each with a slice of pepperoni and some of the cheese. Bake at 425 degrees for 10 to 15 minutes or until golden brown. Serve immediately or store, covered, in the refrigerator.

Yield: 10 servings

It is a deep Girl Scout value that there is always a place for a girl in a troop regardless of her race, ethnicity, ability, or socioeconomic status. Even during the Great Depression in the 1930s, no girl was turned away. To reach this goal, over 300 Girl Scout councils exist to provide Girl Scouting. All United States' territories are reached by Girl Scouts and there are even troops for Girl Scouts from the United States who live overseas with their families.

Favorite Chicken Salad

2 1/2 cups chopped cooked chicken
1 cup finely chopped celery
1 cup seedless grape halves
1 cup chopped walnuts
1 teaspoon minced onion

1 teaspoon salt
1 cup mayonnaise or mayonnaise-
 type salad dressing
1/2 cup whipping cream, whipped

Combine the chicken, celery, grape halves, walnuts, onion and salt in a bowl and toss to mix. Add the mayonnaise and whipped cream and mix well. Chill, covered, until ready to serve. Serve on lettuce-lined serving plates. Garnish with green or black sliced olives and sweet pickle slices.

Yield: 6 servings

To lay a table, spread the tablecloth smoothly and evenly. Put the knives, spoons, forks, and other things also very neatly—but before putting them there see that there is not a speck of dirt on them, no finger-marks or dust.

Although there is a regular way of laying a table, and all tables look much alike when laid, there is a great difference between one laid by a Guide and one laid by any other girl. What is the difference? The "any other girl" puts the knives, forks, and spoons in their correct places as she has been taught to do. The Guide thinks for herself what things will be needed for the meal, how many courses there will be, and therefore how many knives, forks, and spoons, whether pepper will be wanted, or sugar, and puts them on the table accordingly. She uses her wits as well as her hands.

Excerpt from "Girl Guiding" by Lord Baden-Powell, 1938

Seafood Salad

1 (10-ounce) package imitation crab meat
1 to 2 cups shredded Colby Jack cheese
2 medium tomatoes, chopped
1 (5-ounce) can sliced black olives, drained
3 ribs celery, chopped
1 cucumber, chopped
1 (16-ounce) bottle ranch salad dressing
1 head lettuce

Cut the crab meat into pieces. Combine the crab meat, cheese, tomatoes, black olives, celery and cucumber in a bowl.

Add enough of the salad dressing to moisten. Shred the lettuce into a large bowl. Add the crab meat mixture and toss to mix.

Yield: 8 servings

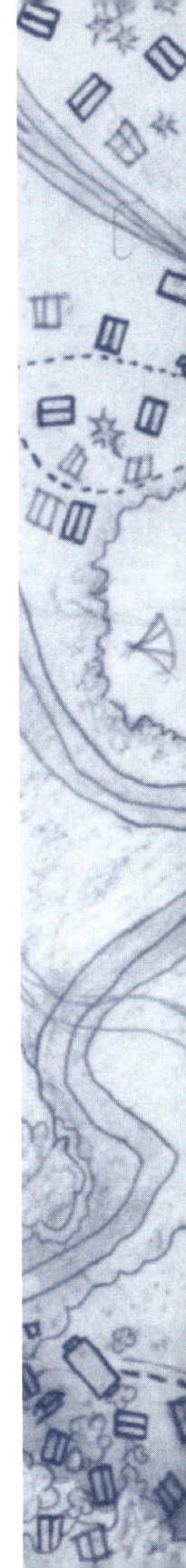

Chinatown Almond Chicken

1 1/2 pounds boneless skinless
 chicken breasts
1 teaspoon ginger
2 teaspoons sugar
1 tablespoon cornstarch
3 tablespoons water
3 tablespoons soy sauce
1/3 cup sherry
1/4 cup vegetable oil
1 cup natural or blanched almonds
2 (6-ounce) packages Chinese pea pods

Cut the chicken into 1/2-inch cubes. Mix the ginger, sugar and cornstarch in a bowl. Add the water, soy sauce and sherry and blend well. Heat the oil in a wok over medium heat. Add the almonds. Sauté for 3 minutes.

Add the chicken. Sauté until cooked through. Add the sherry mixture. Cook until the sauce thickens, stirring constantly. Thaw the pea pods under running water; drain. Add the pea pods to the chicken mixture. Stir-fry until hot and glazed. Serve immediately.

Yield: 4 servings

Note: You may add sliced mushrooms, sliced water chestnuts, bean sprouts and bamboo shoots.

Honey Mustard Chicken

1 tablespoon butter or margarine
4 boneless skinless chicken breasts
1 (10-ounce) can cream of chicken soup
1/4 cup mayonnaise
2 tablespoons honey
1 tablespoon spicy brown mustard
Chopped toasted pecans or walnuts to taste

Melt the butter in a medium skillet over medium-high heat. Add the chicken. Cook for 10 minutes or until brown. Remove the chicken to a warm bowl. Add the soup, mayonnaise, honey and mustard to the pan drippings in the skillet and mix well. Bring to a boil. Return the chicken to the skillet. Reduce the heat to low. Cook, covered, for 5 minutes or until the chicken is cooked through. Sprinkle with pecans. Serve over hot cooked rice.

Yield: 4 servings

Daily Health Rules

Only feed on wholesome fare;
Through your nostrils breathe fresh air;
Clean yourself inside and out;
Twist and bend and run about.

Excerpt from "Girl Guiding" by Lord Baden-Powell, 1938

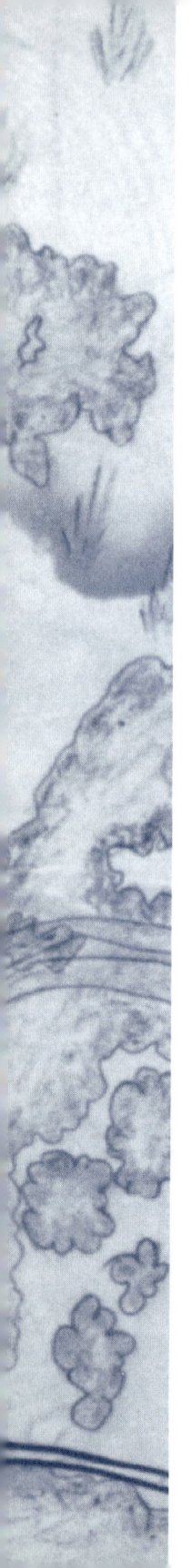

Chicken Julienne

2 boneless chicken breasts
1/2 cup (1 stick) butter
1/2 cup all-purpose flour
1/2 teaspoon lemon juice
Salt and pepper to taste
1 cup heavy cream
1/4 cup shredded Parmesan cheese
  or mozzarella cheese
Paprika to taste

Cut the chicken into large strips. Melt the butter in a shallow dish. Dredge the chicken in the flour. Dip in the melted butter.

Arrange in a single layer in a 9×13-inch glass dish. Sprinkle with the lemon juice. Season with salt and pepper. Pour the cream over the top. Sprinkle with the Parmesan cheese and paprika. Bake at 350 degrees for 20 minutes or until the chicken is cooked through.

Yield: 4 servings

Creamy Chicken and Rice

1 cup uncooked instant rice
1 cup water
1 (15-ounce) can mixed vegetables, drained
1 (10-ounce) can cream of chicken soup
1 (5-ounce) can white chicken, drained
1/4 to 1/2 teaspoon basil
Pinch of pepper

Cook the rice in the water in a saucepan using the package directions. Add the mixed vegetables, soup, chicken, basil and pepper and mix well. Cook until heated through, stirring constantly. Serve with hot biscuits and a fresh garden salad.

Yield: 4 servings

The Six Rules of Health

1. Fresh air
2. Cleanliness
    a. Personal
    b. Surroundings
3. Exercise
4. Food
5. Clothing
6. Rest

Excerpt from "Girl Guiding" by Lord Baden-Powell, 1938

Speedy Paella

2 cups hot water
2 cups frozen chopped cooked chicken
1 cup uncooked long grain rice
1/2 cup green peas
1/2 cup chopped onion
2 teaspoons instant chicken bouillon
1 garlic clove, minced
1/4 teaspoon ground saffron or ground turmeric
1/8 teaspoon ground red pepper
1 (7-ounce) can artichoke hearts
12 ounces frozen cooked shrimp, thawed
1 (2-ounce) jar chopped pimento, drained

Combine the hot water, chicken, rice, peas, onion, bouillon granules, garlic, saffron and red pepper in a large saucepan. Bring to a boil and reduce the heat to low.

Simmer, covered, for 20 minutes. Rinse the artichoke hearts; drain. Cut the artichoke hearts into quarters. Add the artichokes quarters to the rice mixture with the shrimp and pimento. Cook, covered, for 1 to 2 minutes or until the shrimp are heated through.

Yield: 4 servings

Beef and Bean Burritos

1 pound ground beef
1 medium onion, chopped
2 (16-ounce) cans refried beans
1/4 cup salsa
1 teaspoon cumin
1 teaspoon oregano

8 (10-inch) flour tortillas
2 cups shredded Cheddar cheese
Shredded lettuce
2 tomatoes, chopped
Sour cream

Brown the ground beef and onion in a skillet until the ground beef is crumbly; drain. Stir in the refried beans, salsa, cumin and oregano. Cook for 3 to 4 minutes or until heated through and bubbly. Place 1/2 cup of the bean mixture in the center of each tortilla. Sprinkle each with 1/2 tablespoon cheese. Fold two sides together and roll up. Arrange on a baking sheet. Sprinkle each with 1/4 cup cheese. Broil for 2 to 3 minutes or until the cheese melts. Serve on a bed of shredded lettuce with the tomatoes, sour cream and additional salsa.

Yield: 8 servings

Waste

The really orderly Scout has a place for bits. She keeps, for instance, a box of scraps from dress making, a drawer for paper and string, a place for collecting what might be given away. In this way she knows where to turn in a moment for anything that is wanted. 'A place for everything and everything in its place,' which in the end saves time. Waste of time is the worst of waste.

Excerpt from "How Girls Can Help Their Country," The 1913 "Handbook for Girl Scouts," by W. J. Hoxie

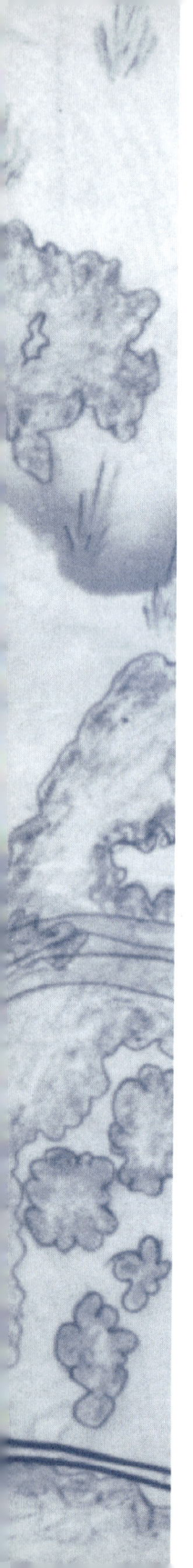

Curly Noodle Ground Beef Dinner

1 pound ground beef or ground turkey
1 (3-ounce) package beef- or pork-flavor ramen noodles
1 (14-ounce) can stewed tomatoes
1 (8-ounce) can whole kernel corn

Brown the ground beef in a skillet, stirring until crumbly; drain. Stir in the seasoning packet from the noodles, undrained tomatoes and undrained corn. Crumble the noodles into the skillet and mix well. Bring to a boil and reduce the heat. Simmer, covered, for 10 minutes or until the noodles are tender.

Yield: 4 servings

Sloppy Joes

2 pounds ground beef
1 (10-ounce) can French onion soup
1 cup ketchup
2 tablespoons brown sugar

Brown the ground beef in a skillet, stirring until crumbly; drain. Add the soup, ketchup and brown sugar and mix well. Bring to a boil and reduce the heat. Simmer for 15 minutes or until the desired consistency.

Yield: 8 servings

Taco Pie

2 (1-crust) refrigerator pie pastries
1 pound ground beef
1 (15-ounce) can spicy chili beans
1/2 cup salsa
1 1/2 cups shredded Cheddar cheese
  or Mexican blend cheese
1 cup shredded lettuce
1/2 cup chopped tomato
Sliced green onions
Sour cream
Sliced black olives
Chopped jalapeños

Unfold 1 of the pie pastries and place in a 9-inch pie plate. Prick the bottom and side with a fork. Flute the edge. Unfold the remaining pie pastry. Cut into thirteen 2-inch triangles. Arrange the triangles around the edge. Bake at 425 degrees for 9 to 11 minutes or until light golden brown. Brown the ground beef in a large skillet, stirring until crumbly; drain. Add the chili beans, salsa and 1 cup of the cheese and mix well.

Cook over low heat for 2 to 3 minutes or until the cheese melts. Spoon into the baked pie shell. Layer the remaining 1/2 cup cheese, lettuce, tomato, green onions, sour cream, black olives and chiles over the ground beef mixture.

Yield: 6 to 8 servings

Spicy Cranberry Pork Stir-Fry

2 tablespoons sherry
1 teaspoon cornstarch
1/4 teaspoon salt
8 ounces boneless lean pork, cut into strips
1 to 2 tablespoons vegetable oil
1/8 teaspoon crushed dried red chiles
1 tablespoon vegetable oil

1 1/2 cups pea pods
1 1/2 cups chopped cranberries
1 (8-ounce) can pineapple chunks, drained
1/4 cup chicken broth
1 teaspoon sesame oil
1 teaspoon cornstarch
1/4 teaspoon sugar
1/4 teaspoon black pepper

Mix the sherry, 1 teaspoon cornstarch and salt in a bowl. Add the pork and mix well. Let stand for 15 minutes. Heat 1 to 2 tablespoons vegetable oil in a wok or skillet. Add the red chiles. Stir-fry for 30 seconds. Add the pork. Stir-fry until the pork is cooked through. Remove from the wok. Add 1 tablespoon vegetable oil if needed and heat. Add the pea pods.

Stir-fry for 1 minute or until tender-crisp. Add the cranberries, pineapple and cooked pork. Stir-fry for 1 minute or until heated through. Mix the chicken broth, sesame oil, 1 teaspoon cornstarch, sugar and black pepper in a bowl. Add to the pork mixture. Stir-fry until the sauce thickens and coats the mixture.

Yield: 4 servings

Note: This recipe provided courtesy of Ocean Spray.

Sausage Bail-Out

1 package smoked sausage or ring bologna
1 green bell pepper, cut into slices or cubes
1 (28-ounce) can diced tomatoes
1 (20-ounce) can pineapple chunks
1 tablespoon cornstarch
1/4 cup water
1 pound medium shell or penne pasta, cooked

Cut the smoked sausage into 1/4-inch rings. Heat the smoked sausage, bell pepper, undrained tomatoes and undrained pineapple in a skillet. Mix the cornstarch with the water in a bowl. Add to the smoked sausage mixture. Cook until the sauce begins to thicken, stirring constantly. Serve immediately over the hot pasta.

Yield: 6 servings

Note: You may add whole kernel corn, mushrooms and/or green beans.

Compare with the requirement today for proficiency badges.

Cook—Must know how to wash up, wait on table, light a fire, lay a table for four, and hand dishes correctly at table. Clean and dress a fowl; clean a fish. How to make a cook-place in the open; make tea, coffee, or cocoa, mix dough and bake bread in oven, and state approximate cost of each dish. Know how to cook two kinds of meat. Boil or roast two kinds of vegetables, potatoes, rice and another vegetable. How to make two salads. How to make a preserve of berries or fruit, or to can them.

Excerpt from "How Girls Can Help Their Country,"
The 1913 "Handbook for Girl Scouts," by W. J. Hoxie

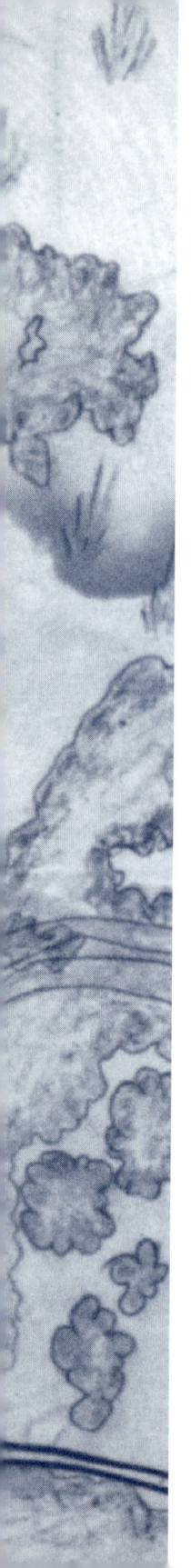

Honey Mustard Kabobs

16 (1/2-inch) zucchini slices
8 bratwurst or smoked Polish sausage, cooked
1 (16-ounce) can whole new potatoes
16 cherry tomatoes
3 tablespoons Dijon mustard
2 tablespoons honey

Microwave the zucchini in a microwave-safe dish on High for 4 minutes or until tender-crisp. Cut the sausage crosswise into thirds. Thread the sausage, potatoes, zucchini and tomatoes alternately onto skewers until all of the ingredients are used.

Mix the Dijon mustard and honey in a bowl. Brush over the kabobs. Place on a rack in a broiler pan. Broil 4 inches from the heat source for 2 minutes. Turn over the kabobs. Brush with the honey-mustard mixture. Broil for 3 minutes longer.

Yield: 4 servings

Artichoke Pesto Pasta

1 cup finely chopped onion
3 tablespoons clarified margarine
1 cup chopped fresh tomatoes
6 large canned artichoke hearts, drained, cut into quarters

1 pound pasta spirals, cooked
1 cup pesto
1/3 cup freshly grated Parmesan cheese
1/2 cup pine nuts, toasted

Sauté the onion in the margarine in a large saucepan over medium heat until transparent. Add the tomatoes and artichoke hearts. Sauté until heated through. Add the pasta and pesto gradually, stirring constantly. Cook until heated through, stirring constantly. Sprinkle with Parmesan cheese and pine nuts.

Yield: 4 to 6 servings

Compare with the requirement today for proficiency badges.

Matron Housekeeper—Know how to use a vacuum cleaner. How to stain and polish hardwood floors. How to clean wire window screens. How to put away fur and flannels. How to clean glass, kitchen utensils, brass, and silverware. Know three different cuts of meat, and prices of each. Know season for chief fruits and vegetables, fish and game. Know how flour, sugar, rice, cereals and vegetables are sold; whether by package, pound or bulk, quarts.

Excerpt from "How Girls Can Help Their Country,"
The 1913 "Handbook for Girl Scouts," by W. J. Hoxie

ROSSE COUNTY
SACAJAWEA
RIVER
MINNEHAHA
DINNING LODGE
PARKING LOT
ROAD
POOL
MARINUKA
COOK OUT
COOK OUT
ROAD

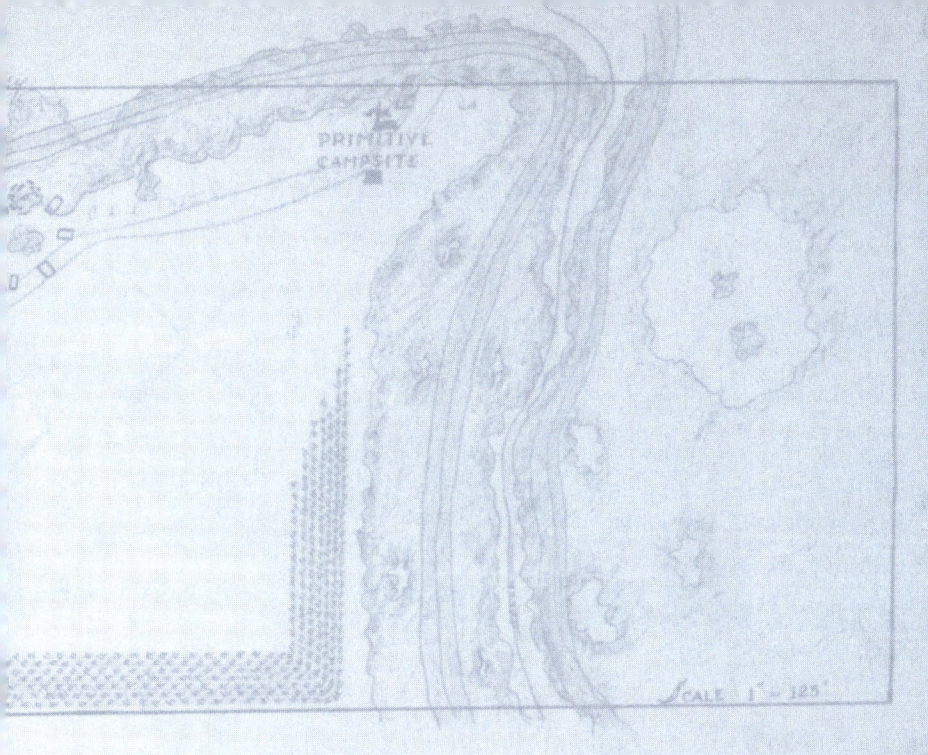

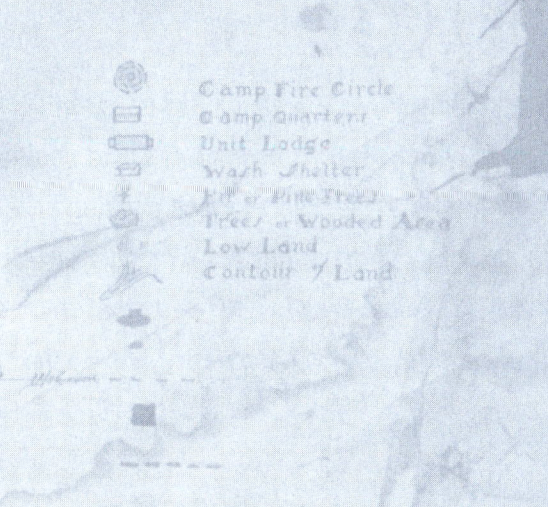

Girl Scout Desserts
And Other Sweet Things

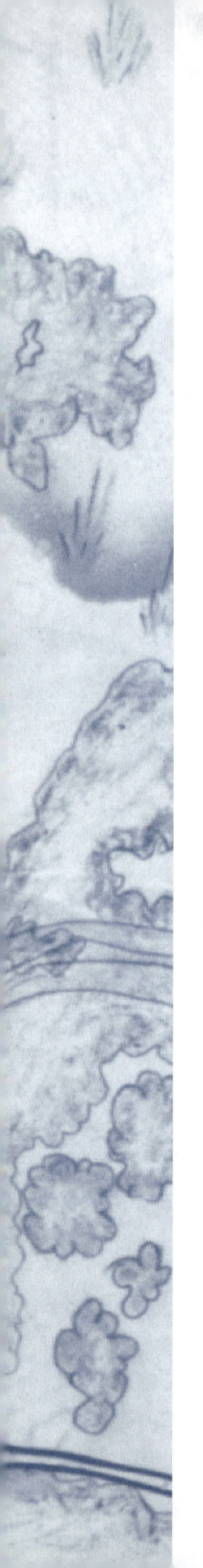

Original Home-Baked Girl Scout Cookies

(Circa 1922)

1 cup (2 sticks) butter or margarine, softened
1 cup sugar
2 eggs, beaten
2 tablespoons milk
1 teaspoon vanilla extract
2 cups all-purpose flour
2 teaspoons baking powder
Sugar crystals to taste

Cream the butter and sugar in a mixing bowl until light and fluffy. Beat in the eggs. Add the milk, vanilla, flour and baking powder and mix well. Roll the dough thin on a lightly floured surface. Cut into trefoil shapes. Arrange on nonstick cookie sheets. Sprinkle with sugar crystals. Bake at 350 degrees for 8 minutes or until golden brown. Cool on wire racks.

Yield: 2 dozen

Each year, everyone has the pleasure of meeting a Girl Scout at his or her door who has a simple question—"How many Girl Scout cookies would you like to buy?" Funds raised from the sale of these cookies have provided millions of girls with amazing opportunities. The famous Girl Scout cookies were introduced to the La Crosse area in 1931—at that time, a dozen cookies could be purchased for as little as twenty cents a box.

Cranberry Cookies

3 cups sifted all-purpose flour
1 teaspoon baking powder
1/4 teaspoon baking soda
1/2 teaspoon salt
1/2 cup (1 stick) butter or margarine, softened
1 cup sugar
3/4 cup packed brown sugar
1/4 cup milk
2 tablespoons orange juice
1 egg
2 1/2 cups coarsely chopped fresh cranberries
1 cup chopped nuts

Sift the flour, baking powder, baking soda and salt together. Cream the butter, sugar and brown sugar in a mixing bowl until light and fluffy.

Beat in the milk, orange juice and egg. Add the flour mixture and beat well. Stir in the cranberries and chopped nuts. Drop by teaspoonfuls onto greased cookie sheets. Bake at 375 degrees for 10 to 15 minutes or until golden brown. Cool on wire racks.

Yield: 12 dozen

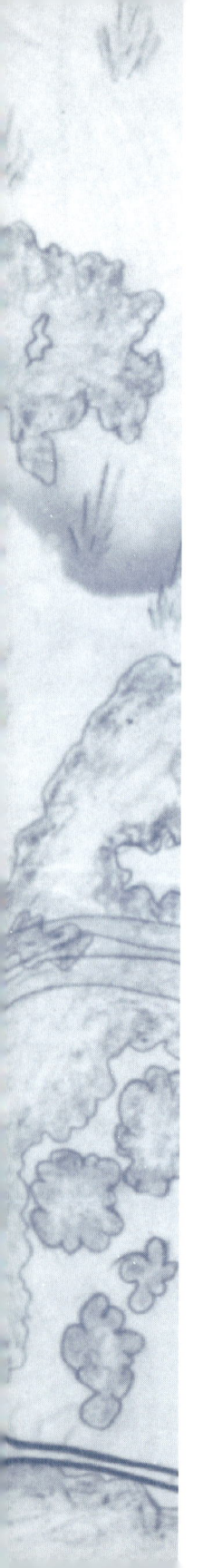

Cranberry Cookies with Orange Glaze

2 1/2 cups all-purpose flour
3/4 teaspoon baking powder
1/4 teaspoon baking soda
1/2 teaspoon salt
1 teaspoon cinnamon
1/2 cup (1 stick) butter or
  margarine, softened
3/4 cup sugar
1/2 cup packed brown sugar

1 teaspoon vanilla extract
1/3 cup milk
1 egg
1 cup chopped toasted walnuts
2 teaspoons grated orange zest
2 1/2 cups fresh cranberries,
  coarsely chopped
Orange Glaze (below)

Sift the flour, baking powder, baking soda, salt and cinnamon together. Cream the butter, sugar, brown sugar and vanilla in a mixing bowl until light and fluffy. Beat in the milk and egg. Add the flour mixture and mix well. Stir in the walnuts, orange zest and cranberries. Arrange 1 level tablespoonful at a time 2 inches apart on well-greased cookie sheets. Bake at 375 degrees for 15 minutes. Brush with Orange Glaze. Bake for 5 minutes longer. Cool on wire racks.

Yield: 5 dozen

Orange Glaze

1/2 cup sugar
1/4 cup orange juice
1 teaspoon grated orange zest

Combine the sugar, orange juice and orange zest in a small bowl and mix well.

Yield: 3/4 cup

Lace Cookies in a Jar

1 1/2 cups all-purpose flour
2 cups rolled oats
1/2 cup packed brown sugar
1/2 cup sugar
1/2 cup chopped nuts

Layer the flour, oats, brown sugar, sugar and nuts in the order listed in a sterilized 1-quart jar with a lid. Secure the jar with the lid. Cover the lid with a 5-inch circle of cloth. Attach the following directions to the jar with yarn and give as a gift.

For Lace Cookies, add 1 cup shortening, 1/2 teaspoon baking soda dissolved in 1/4 cup hot water and 2 teaspoons vanilla extract to the cookie mix and mix well. Shape into balls and arrange on lightly greased cookie sheets. Flatten each with the tines of a fork. Bake at 375 degrees for 8 to 10 minutes or until golden brown. Cool on wire racks.

Yield: 2 dozen

For over seventy years, Girl Scout cookie activities have helped girls learn invaluable skills, such as decision-making, money management, and delivering on a promise. These activities are directly related to our mission of helping all girls realize their full potential and become strong, confident, and resourceful citizens.

Excerpt from "What We Stand For," GSUSA 2001

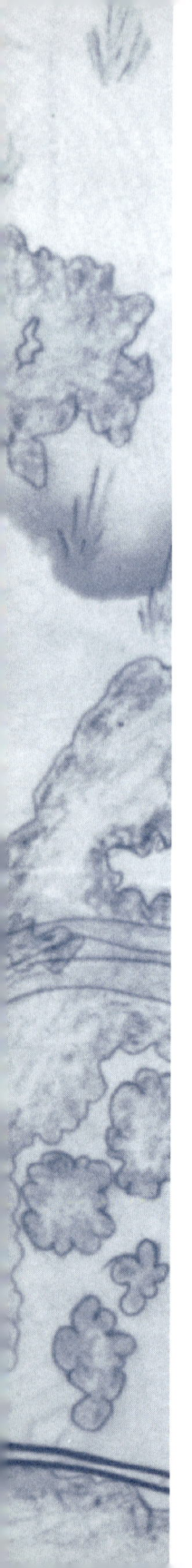

Caramel Bars

2 cups all-purpose flour
2 cups old-fashioned oats
1 cup packed brown sugar
1 teaspoon baking soda
1/4 teaspoon salt
1 cup (2 sticks) butter, melted
2 cups (12 ounces) chocolate chips
1 cup caramel ice cream topping
1/3 cup all-purpose flour

Combine 2 cups flour, oats, brown sugar, baking soda and salt in a large bowl. Stir in the butter. Reserve 1 cup of the crumb mixture. Press the remaining crumb mixture into a greased 9×13-inch baking dish. Bake at 350 degrees for 15 minutes. Remove from the oven. Sprinkle with the chocolate chips.

Mix the caramel ice cream topping and 1/3 cup flour in a small bowl. Drizzle over the chocolate chips. Sprinkle with the reserved crumb mixture. Bake at 350 degrees for 20 to 25 minutes or until light brown. Cool slightly and cut into bars.

Yield: 3 dozen

Davy Crockett Bars

1 cup (2 sticks) butter, softened
1 cup packed brown sugar
1 teaspoon vanilla extract
1 teaspoon salt
1 teaspoon baking powder
1 cup (6 ounces) chocolate chips

1 cup sugar
3 eggs
2 cups all-purpose flour
1 teaspoon baking soda
2 cups quick-cooking oats
1 cup chopped nuts or raisins

Combine the butter, brown sugar, vanilla, salt, baking powder, chocolate chips, sugar, eggs, flour, baking soda, oats and nuts in the order listed in a large bowl, mixing well after each addition. Press onto an ungreased cookie sheet. Bake at 350 degrees for 25 to 30 minutes or until golden brown. Cool slightly and cut into bars.

Yield: 3 dozen

Each troop or group that sells cookies earns money for its treasury and plans how to spend that money to achieve its goals. The proceeds are used for field trips, service projects, and other activities. In addition, Girl Scouts can earn age-appropriate proficiency awards as part of their experience with cookie activities.

Excerpt from "What We Stand For," GSUSA 2001

Kit Kat Bars

Waverly or club crackers
1 cup (2 sticks) butter
1 cup packed brown sugar
1/3 cup sugar
2 cups graham cracker crumbs
1/2 cup milk
1/2 cup (3 ounces) chocolate chips
1/2 cup (3 ounces) butterscotch chips
2/3 cup peanut butter

Line a greased 9×13-inch baking pan with crackers. Combine the butter, brown sugar, sugar, graham cracker crumbs and milk in a medium saucepan. Bring to a boil. Boil for 3 to 5 minutes, stirring constantly.

Pour 1/3 of the sauce in the prepared pan. Arrange a layer of crackers over the sauce. Pour 1/2 of the remaining sauce over the crackers. Arrange another layer of crackers over the sauce. Pour the remaining sauce over the layers. Top with another layer of crackers.

Melt the chocolate chips, butterscotch chips and peanut butter in a saucepan, stirring constantly. Pour over the layers. Chill, covered, until the chocolate hardens. Cut into bars.

Yield: 3 dozen

Rhubarb Dream Bars

2 cups all-purpose flour
1/2 cup plus 2 tablespoons sugar
1 cup (2 sticks) butter, softened
4 eggs, beaten
2 cups sugar
1/2 cup all-purpose flour
4 cups chopped rhubarb

Combine 2 cups flour, 1/2 cup plus 2 tablespoons sugar and butter in a bowl and mix well. Spread in a nonstick 9×13-inch baking pan. Bake at 350 degrees for 15 minutes. Remove from the oven. Beat the eggs, 2 cups sugar and 1/2 cup flour in a bowl. Stir in the rhubarb. Pour over the baked layer. Bake for 30 minutes. Cool slightly and cut into bars.

Yield: 18 to 21 servings

"**C**ookie Revenue" helps to provide the financial assistance needed to make Girl Scouting available for all girls, to fund special events and other program opportunities, to keep event/camp fees for all members to a minimum, to improve and maintain camp and other activity sites, and to recruit and train volunteer leaders.

Excerpt from "What We Stand For," GSUSA 2001

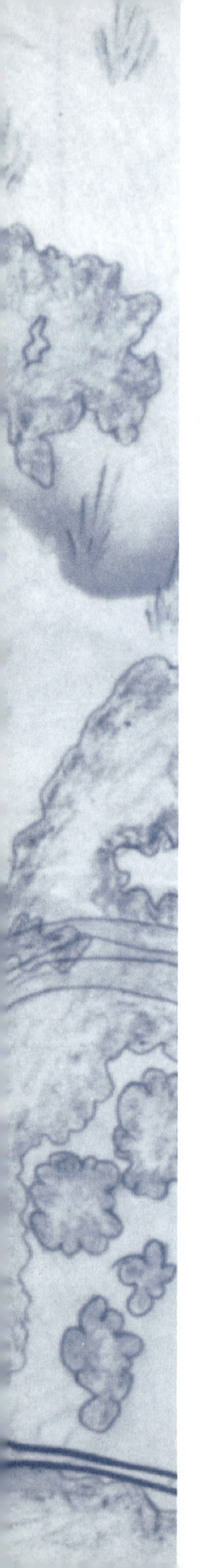

Special K Bars

1 cup light corn syrup
1 cup sugar
1 1/2 cups peanut butter
6 cups Special K cereal
1 cup (8 ounces) butterscotch chips
1 cup (8 ounces) chocolate chips

Bring the corn syrup and sugar to a boil in a saucepan. Remove from the heat. Add the peanut butter and mix until smooth. Stir in the cereal. Press in a 9×13-inch dish. Microwave the butterscotch chips and chocolate chips in a microwave-safe dish until softened; stir until smooth. Spread over the top of the cereal mixture. Cool slightly and cut into bars.

Yield: 3 dozen

Girl Scout Crunchy Caramel Apples

12 small apples
1 (16-ounce) package caramels
12 Girl Scout Do-si-dos, finely chopped

Insert a wooden stick into the top of each apple. Unwrap the caramels and place in a double boiler. Melt over hot water, stirring frequently. Dip the apples into the melted caramel, using a spoon to spread evenly over the whole apple and allowing the excess to drip off. Dip the bottoms of the apples immediately into the cookie crumbs. Arrange the apples cookie-coated side down on waxed paper. Let stand for 30 minutes or until firm.

Yield: 12 servings

Old-Fashioned Vanilla Ice Cream

1 cup plus 2 tablespoons sugar
3 tablespoons all-purpose flour
1/4 teaspoon salt
2 1/2 cups milk

2 eggs, beaten
2 cups heavy cream
1/2 tablespoon vanilla extract
1 vanilla bean, ground

Combine the sugar, flour and salt in a 2-quart saucepan. Add the milk gradually, stirring constantly. Cook over medium heat for 15 minutes or until thickened, stirring constantly. Stir 1 cup of the hot mixture into the beaten eggs. Add to the remaining hot mixture, stirring constantly. Cook for 1 minute, stirring constantly. Remove from the heat. Chill, covered, for 2 hours. Mix the cream, vanilla extract and ground vanilla bean in a large bowl. Add the chilled mixture and beat with a whisk to blend. Pour into an ice cream freezer container. Freeze using the manufacturer's directions.

Yield: 8 servings

Girl Scout Week

Girl Scouts across the country celebrate the week that includes March 12 as "Girl Scout Week" because March 12 is the anniversary of the founding of Girl Scouting in the United States. This week was designated by the National Council as Girl Scout Week in October 1953. The week begins with the Sunday on or prior to March 12, and concludes the following Saturday. During Girl Scout Week it is customary for Girl Scout troops or groups to do a service project and to learn more about the history of Girl Scouting, about the life of founder Juliette Gordon Low, or about the government in their own communities.

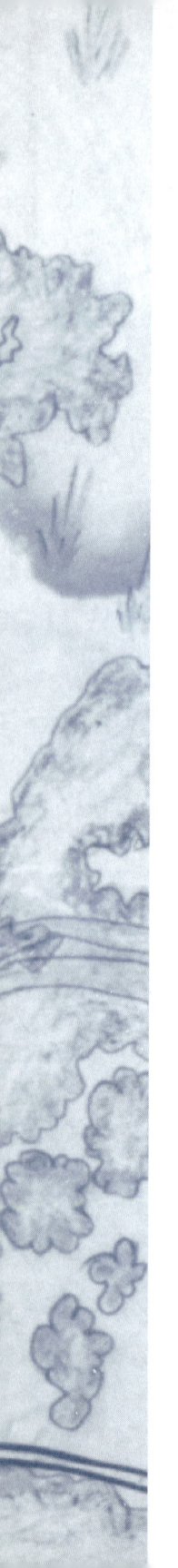

Favorite Apple Crisp

4 cups sliced peeled apples
3/4 cup packed brown sugar
1/2 cup all-purpose flour
1/2 cup rolled oats
1 teaspoon ground cinnamon
1/4 teaspoon ground allspice
1/3 cup butter

Arrange the apples in a greased 8×8-inch baking dish. Combine the brown sugar, flour, oats, cinnamon and allspice in a bowl. Cut in the butter until crumbly. Sprinkle over the apples. Bake at 375 degrees for 30 to 35 minutes or until the apples are tender. Serve warm with ice cream.

Yield: 4 to 6 servings

Banana Split Dessert

2 cups graham cracker crumbs
1/2 cup (1 stick) butter, melted
2 eggs, pasteurized
2 cups confectioners' sugar
1 cup (2 sticks) butter, softened
5 or 6 bananas, sliced
1 (20-ounce) can crushed pineapple, drained
16 ounces whipped topping
1 (4-ounce) jar maraschino cherries, drained
Chopped nuts (optional)

Mix the cracker crumbs and 1/2 cup butter in a bowl. Press into a 9×13-inch dish. Beat the eggs, confectioners' sugar and 1 cup butter at medium speed in a mixing bowl for 15 minutes. Spread in the prepared dish. Layer the bananas and pineapple over the filling. Spread the whipped topping over the top. Sprinkle with the maraschino cherries and nuts. Chill, covered, in the refrigerator.

Yield: 20 to 24 servings

Scouting During World War II

In the 1940s, I was a Brownie and Girl Scout in Troop 15 at the Training School (later called the Campus School) in La Crosse. For the war effort, we went door-to-door in assigned areas collecting rags. One afternoon in April of 1945, a lady in a house on North Losey Boulevard handed me a bag of rags to put in my wagon and told me President Roosevelt had died. She was very upset and I went right home to ask my mother if it was true.

I remember wondering how long "the duration" would be. Toilet paper rolls were flattened to fit more rolls in a carton. Each roll said the crushing would continue "for the duration." Clothes, sugar, meat, and butter were rationed. We had ration books and tokens. Cream was not rationed, so my mother made our butter by beating the cream in the Mix Master until butter formed.

The speed limit was thirty-five miles per hour, so needless to say, car trips were not frequent. The gas card always asked, "Is this trip really necessary?" Only for my father's work!

The next August 1945, I attended Camp Decorah for one week, staying in a cabin (the older girls stayed in tents beyond the swimming pond). Early one morning, I was helping in the dining hall doing "capers" and the adults were very excited about something that fell from the sky right on Japan— I thought the "miracle" was a meteorite. It was the first atomic bomb.

Alice Engelhard Gassere, Mindoro, Wisconsin

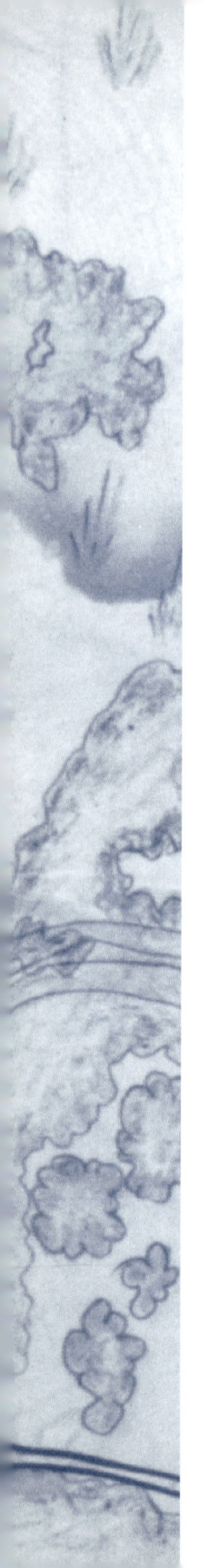

Fruit with Lime

1/2 small melon, peeled
1 small cantaloupe, peeled
1 pint strawberries, hulled
1 large kiwifruit, peeled
12 ounces seedless red grapes

12 ounces seedless green grapes
1/2 cup blueberries
1/3 cup frozen limeade concentrate, thawed

Cut the melon, cantaloupe, strawberries and kiwifruit into bite-size pieces. Combine with the red grapes, green grapes and blueberries in a large bowl. Drizzle with the limeade concentrate. Chill, covered, until ready to serve.

Yield: 8 to 12 servings

Home Life: Sanitation

Fresh air is your great friend, it will help you to fight disease better than anything else. Open all your windows as often as you can, so that air may get into every nook and corner. Never keep an unused room shut up...Disease germs, poisonous gases, mildew, insects, dust and dirt have it all their own way in stale, used-up air.

You do not like to wash in water other people have used, but it is far worse to breathe air other people have breathed.... The night air in large towns is purer than the day air, and both in town and country you should sleep with your window open if you want to be healthy.

Excerpt from "How Girls Can Help Their Country,"
the 1913 "Handbook for Girl Scouts," by W. J. Hoxie

Girl Scout Levitating Layers

1/2 cup all-purpose flour
1/2 cup (1 stick) margarine, melted
1 package Girl Scout Samoas, cut into pieces
1 cup confectioners' sugar
8 ounces cream cheese, softened
1/2 cup whipped topping
1 (6-ounce) package chocolate instant pudding mix
2 1/2 cups cold milk
1/2 cup whipped topping

Mix the flour, margarine and cookie pieces in a bowl. Pat into a baking dish. Bake at 325 degrees for 25 minutes. Remove from the oven and cool.

Beat the confectioners' sugar, cream cheese and 1/2 cup whipped topping in a mixing bowl until smooth and creamy. Spread over the cooled crust.

Mix the pudding mix and milk in a bowl until smooth and thick. Spread over the cream cheese layer. Spread 1/2 cup whipped topping over the top. Chill, covered, for 30 to 60 minutes before serving.

Yield: 12 servings

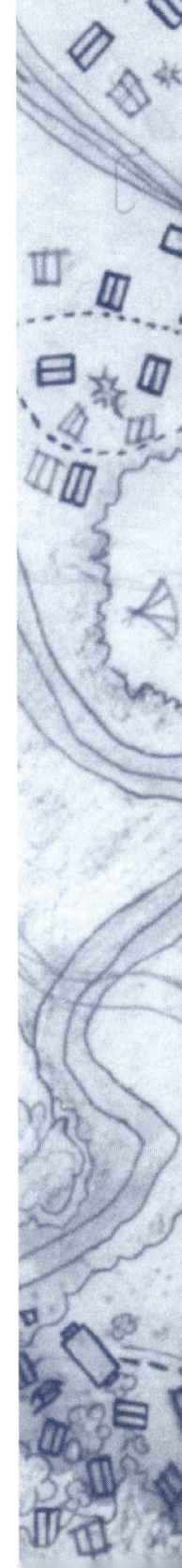

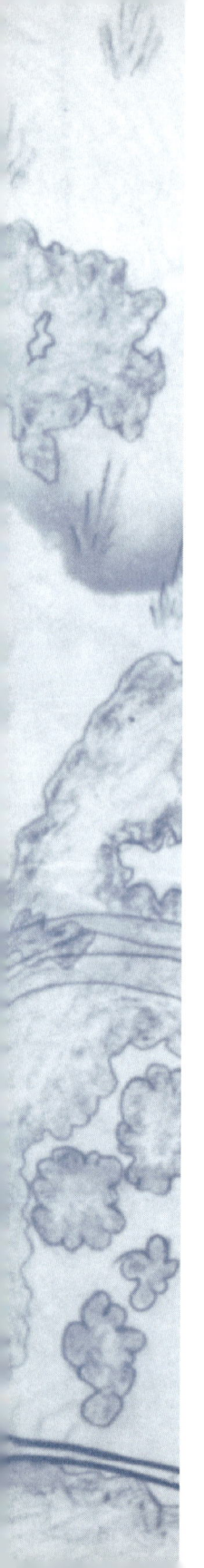

Girl Scout Mint Delight

1 package Girl Scout Thin Mints, crushed
3 tablespoons butter or margarine, melted
8 ounces cream cheese, softened
1 cup whipped topping
2 (6-ounce) packages chocolate instant pudding mix
3 cups cold milk
3 cups whipped topping

Reserve 1/4 cup of the cookie crumbs for the top. Combine the remaining cookie crumbs and butter in a bowl and mix well. Press into a 9×13-inch dish. Chill in the refrigerator. Beat the cream cheese and 1 cup whipped topping in a mixing bowl until smooth. Spread in the prepared dish.

Chill, covered, for 15 to 20 minutes. Mix the pudding mix and milk in a bowl until smooth and thick. Pour over the cream cheese layer. Chill, covered, for 1 hour or until ready to serve. Spread 3 cups whipped topping over the top. Sprinkle with the reserved cookie crumbs.

Yield: 10 to 12 servings

The Girl Scout Purpose

The purpose of Girl Scouting is to inspire girls with the highest ideals of character, conduct, patriotism, and service that they may become happy and resourceful citizens.

Excerpt from "What We Stand For," GSUSA 2001

Oreo Cheesecake

1 cup crushed Oreo cookies (about 12 cookies)
1 tablespoon butter or margarine, melted
32 ounces cream cheese, softened
1 cup sugar
1 teaspoon vanilla extract
4 eggs
20 Oreo cookies, cut into quarters

Combine the crushed cookies and butter in a bowl and mix well. Press into a 9-inch springform pan. Bake at 325 degrees for 10 minutes.

Beat the cream cheese, sugar and vanilla in a mixing bowl at medium speed until blended. Add the eggs. Beat at low speed until blended. Stir in the cookie quarters. Pour into the prepared pan.

Bake at 325 degrees for 1 hour or until the center is almost set. Loosen the cheesecake from the edge of the pan. Let stand until cool. Remove the side of the pan. Chill, covered, for 4 to 12 hours. Garnish with whipped topping and additional Oreo cookies.

Yield: 12 servings

Note: Bake the crust at 300 degrees for 10 minutes and the filling for 1 hour, if using a dark nonstick springform pan.

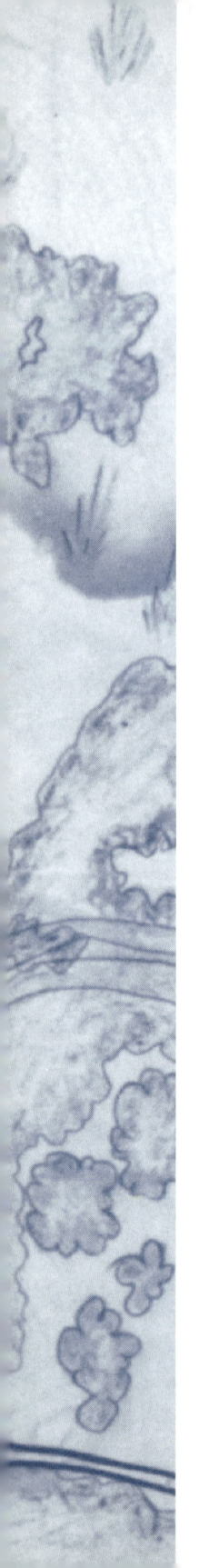

Applesauce Cake

3 cups all-purpose flour
1 tablespoon baking soda
1/2 teaspoon salt
1/2 tablespoon ground nutmeg
1 tablespoon ground cinnamon
1 teaspoon ground cloves
2 1/2 cups applesauce
2 tablespoons corn syrup
1 cup shortening
2 cups sugar
2 eggs
1 cup raisins
1 cup chopped walnuts or pecans

Sift the flour, baking soda, salt, nutmeg, cinnamon and cloves together. Mix the applesauce and corn syrup in a bowl.

Cream the shortening in a mixing bowl until light. Add the sugar and eggs and beat well. Add the flour mixture and applesauce mixture alternately, beating well after each addition. Fold in the raisins and walnuts. Pour into a greased 11×14-inch cake pan. Bake at 300 degrees for 1 1/2 hours.

Yield: 15 to 20 servings

The Best Chocolate Cake

2 cups all-purpose flour
6 tablespoons (heaping) baking cocoa
1 3/4 teaspoons baking soda
1 1/2 to 2 cups sugar
1/2 cup milk
1/2 teaspoon vinegar
1 cup canola oil
2 eggs, lightly beaten
2 teaspoons vanilla extract
1 cup boiling water

Grease a bundt pan and sprinkle with some baking cocoa. Combine the flour, 6 tablespoons baking cocoa, baking soda and sugar in a large mixing bowl. Mix the milk and vinegar in a bowl. Add the canola oil, eggs and vanilla and mix well. Add to the flour mixture. Add the boiling water. Beat for 2 minutes. Pour into the prepared pan. Bake at 350 degrees for 30 to 40 minutes or until the cake tests done. Remove from the oven. Cool in the pan for 10 minutes. Invert onto a cake plate to cool completely.

Yield: 16 servings

---

*S*our milk need not be wasted. Sour milk will clean ink or fruit stains, and in washing it bleaches linen. Yellowed linen should soak in it, so should spoons and forks. Sour milk cleanses oil-cloth as well as women's faces and hands.

Excerpt from "How Girls Can Help Their Country," the 1913 "Handbook for Girl Scouts," by W. J. Hoxie

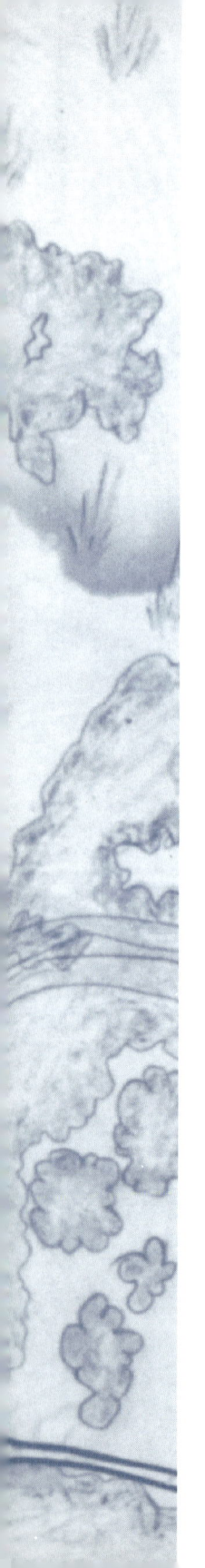

Cherry Chocolate Cake

1 (2-layer) package fudge cake mix
1 (21-ounce) can cherry pie filling
1 teaspoon almond extract
2 eggs
Chocolate Frosting (below)

Combine the cake mix, pie filling, almond extract and eggs in a large bowl and mix well. Pour into a greased 9×13-inch cake pan. Bake at 350 degrees for 35 minutes. Remove from the oven and cool in the pan. Spread the Chocolate Frosting over the top of the cooled cake.

Yield: 15 servings

Chocolate Frosting

1 cup sugar
5 tablespoons butter
1/2 cup milk
1 cup (6-ounces) semisweet chocolate chips

Bring the sugar, butter and milk to a boil in a saucepan. Boil for 1 minute, stirring constantly. Remove from the heat. Add the chocolate chips and beat until smooth.

Yield: 1 1/2 cups

Ice Cream Cone Cakes

1 (2-layer) package favorite
  cake mix
12 flat-bottomed waffle
  ice cream cones

Favorite frosting
Favorite Girl Scout cookies
Candy or nuts

Prepare the cake mix batter using the package directions. Pour a scant 1/4 cup batter into each cone, filling about 1/2 full. Do not fill too full so a nice round top will form. Arrange on a baking sheet. Bake at 400 degrees for 15 to 18 minutes or until the cakes test done. Let cool. Spread the frosting over the tops of the cooled cakes. Decorate as desired with Girl Scout cookies and candy or nuts.

Yield: 12 servings

Girl Scouts: Who We Are

Girl Scouts is the world's preeminent organization dedicated solely to girls—all girls—where, in an accepting and nurturing environment, girls build character and skills for success in the real world. In partnership with committed adults, girls develop qualities that will serve them all their lives—like strong values, a social conscience, and conviction about their own potential and self-worth.

In Girl Scouts, girls discover the fun, friendship, and power of girls together. Through the many enriching experiences provided by Girl Scouting, they grow courageous and strong.

Excerpt from "What We Stand For," GSUSA 2001

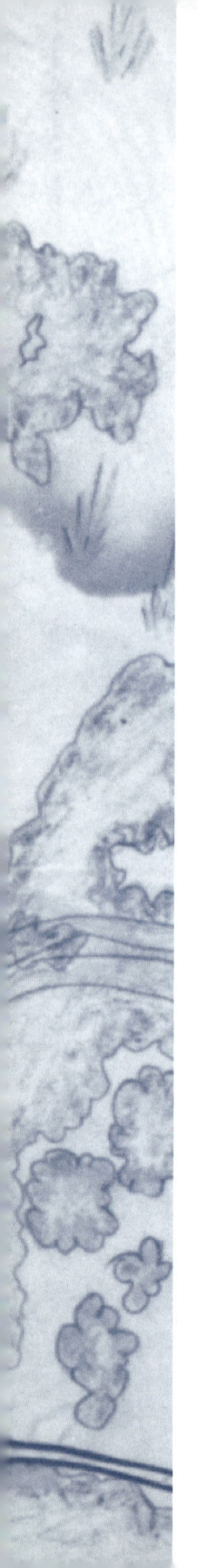

Girl Scout Strawberry Angel Surprise

    1 package angel food cake mix
    1 tube Girl Scout Trefoils
    3 cups whipping cream
    1/2 cup confectioners' sugar
    2 cups chopped, drained, thawed, frozen unsweetened strawberries
    10 whole strawberries

Prepare and bake the cake using the package directions for a tube pan. Remove from the oven and invert on a funnel to cool completely. Loosen the cake from the side of the pan. Invert onto a cake plate.

Reserve 10 whole cookies. Break the remaining cookies into small pieces. Beat the whipping cream and confectioners' sugar in a mixing bowl until soft peaks form. Fold in the chopped strawberries. Combine 2 1/2 cups of the strawberry mixture and broken cookies in a bowl.

Split the cake horizontally into 3 equal portions. Spread 1/2 of the cookie cream mixture on the bottom layer. Add the next cake layer. Spread with the remaining cookie cream mixture. Add the remaining cake layer. Spread the remaining strawberry mixture over the top and side of the cake.

Cut 5 of the reserved cookies into halves. Crush the remaining reserved cookies. Alternate the cookie halves and whole strawberries around the bottom on the side of the cake. Sprinkle the crushed cookies over the top.

Yield: 15 servings

Double-Good Blueberry Pie

3/4 cup sugar
3 tablespoons cornstarch
1/8 teaspoon salt
1/4 cup water
2 cups blueberries

1 tablespoon butter
1 tablespoon lemon juice
2 cups blueberries
1 baked (9-inch) pie shell

Combine the sugar, cornstarch and salt in a saucepan. Add the water and 2 cups blueberries. Bring to a boil over medium heat. Cook until thickened and clear, stirring constantly. The mixture will be thick.

Remove from the heat. Stir in the butter and lemon juice. Let stand until cool. Arrange 2 cups blueberries in the baked pie shell. Add the cooled blueberry mixture. Chill, covered, until ready to serve. Serve with whipped cream.

Yield: 6 to 8 servings

Compare this requirement for a Proficiency Badge in Health with the requirement of today.

Health—Do not chew gum. Eat no sweets, candy, or cake between meals for three months. Drink nothing but water for a year (except tea, coffee, chocolate, or cocoa). Walk a mile daily for three months. Sleep with open window. Take a bath or run all over with a wet towel daily for three months.

Excerpt from "How Girls Can Help Their Country," the 1913 "Handbook for Girl Scouts," by W. J. Hoxie

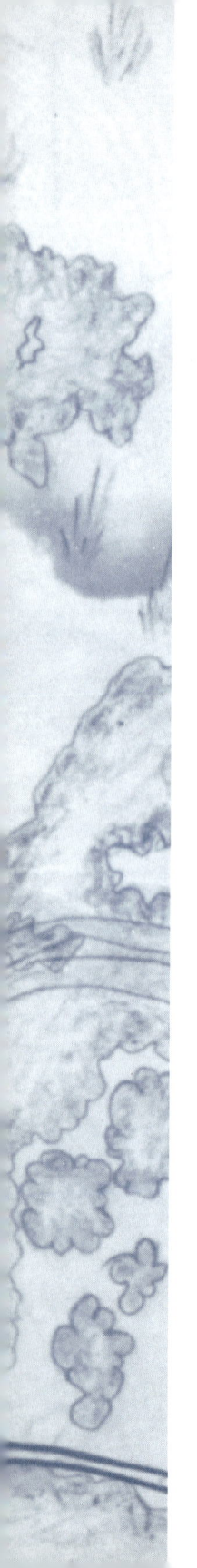

Girl Scout Café au Mint Chocolate Pie

2 pints coffee ice cream
1 1/2 tubes Girl Scout Thin Mint cookies

1/2 cup (3 ounces) semisweet chocolate chips
3 tablespoons heavy cream

Soften the ice cream in the refrigerator for 4 hours or at room temperature for 1 hour. Grease a 9-inch pie plate with margarine. Process the cookies in a food processor until crumbly. Press into the prepared pie plate. Bake at 350 degrees for 10 minutes. Let cool.

Fill the cooled pie shell with the ice cream. Cover with waxed paper. Freeze until firm. Melt the chocolate chips and cream in a small saucepan over low heat, stirring constantly. Spread over the top of the pie. Return to the freezer. Freeze until firm.

Yield: 6 to 8 servings

Girl Scout Southern Peanut Butter Pie

1 package Girl Scout Tagalongs
1 (4-ounce) package vanilla instant pudding mix

1 1/2 cups cold milk
1/3 cup peanut butter

Process the cookies in a blender or food processor until ground. Press into a 9-inch pie plate. Prepare the pudding mix using the package directions, using 1 1/2 cups milk. Stir in the peanut butter. Pour into the prepared pie plate. Chill, covered, until ready to serve. Garnish with whipped topping and crushed peanuts.

Yield: 6 to 8 servings

I remember Hope Kumm very well and what she has done for Girl Scouting. When I was in Girl Scouts we would meet after school at the home of my Scout leader, Mrs. Skundberg. She was a wonderful leader and instructor for earning badges.

I went to Girl Scout camp at Camp Decorah in August, since that was the time the boys weren't using the camp. I remember the smell of the pine trees and their needles, campfires in the evening and singing songs. We stayed in cabins the first couple of years of camping. We had four girls in one cabin and about six cabins to a unit. Each cabin was named after a bird. Our cabin was named The Bluebird. As we got older we slept in tents.

I also remember eating in the mess hall. There were times I never cared for the food that was served. You learned to clean your plate and break your bread into four pieces before putting it in your mouth.

I will always enjoy the memories of Girl Scouting where I learned to be prepared at all times.

Joan Johnson, La Crosse, Wisconsin

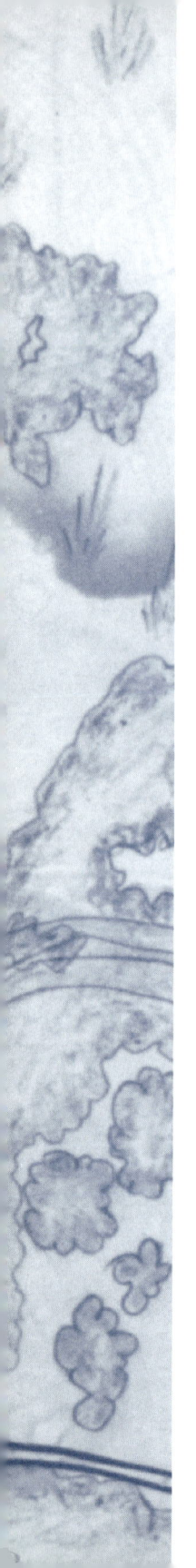

Girl Scout Super Samoa Surprise

1 package Girl Scout Samoas
3/4 cup flaked coconut
2 (4-ounce) packages coconut cream instant
  pudding mix
3 1/2 cups milk
1 ounce bittersweet chocolate
1 teaspoon butter
1 teaspoon cream

Break up the cookies into a food processor. Process until the cookies are evenly crumbled. Press into a 10-inch pie plate. Chill, covered, for 1 hour or longer.

Spread the coconut on a baking sheet. Bake at 325 degrees for about 10 minutes or until evenly brown, stirring every 2 minutes.

Prepare the pudding mix using the package directions, using 3 1/2 cups milk. Pour into the prepared pie plate. Sprinkle with the toasted coconut. Chill in the refrigerator. Microwave the chocolate in a microwave-safe dish on Medium for 1 minute. Add the butter.

Microwave on Medium for 30 to 60 seconds; stir to blend. Repeat the process until the chocolate is completely melted and mixed with the butter. Add the cream and mix well. Drizzle over the top of the pie or place in a decorating bag and pipe any design you wish over the pie. Chill, covered, for 3 to 12 hours.

Yield: 6 to 8 servings

Strawberry Glaze Pie

6 cups fresh strawberries
1 cup water
3/4 cup sugar
3 tablespoons cornstarch
5 drops (about) of red food coloring
1 baked (9-inch) pie shell

Rinse the strawberries and remove the hulls. Place 1 cup of the smallest strawberries in a saucepan and crush. Add the water. Cook for 2 minutes. Strain the mixture, reserving the juice and discarding the solids. Mix the sugar and cornstarch in a saucepan. Stir in the reserved strawberry juice. Cook over medium heat until thickened and clear, stirring constantly. Add the food coloring and mix well. Spread 1/4 cup of the glaze on the bottom and side of the pie shell. Arrange 1/2 of the whole strawberries stem side down in the prepared pie shell. Spoon 1/2 of the remaining glaze over the strawberries, coating well. Arrange the remaining strawberries over the top. Coat with the remaining glaze. Chill, covered, for 3 to 4 hours.

Yield: 6 to 8 servings

Camping offered many new opportunities for the Girl Scouts in our region. As one Girl Scout leader from West Salem recalls, "the ole swimming hole at Lake Neshonic offered but limited opportunities for swimming, but the lovely Lake Como near Houston, Minnesota, was greatly enjoyed by the girls. They also learned about bird and flower life during a nature hike and gathered around a campfire to tell stories and sing songs—a great deal was learned by all."

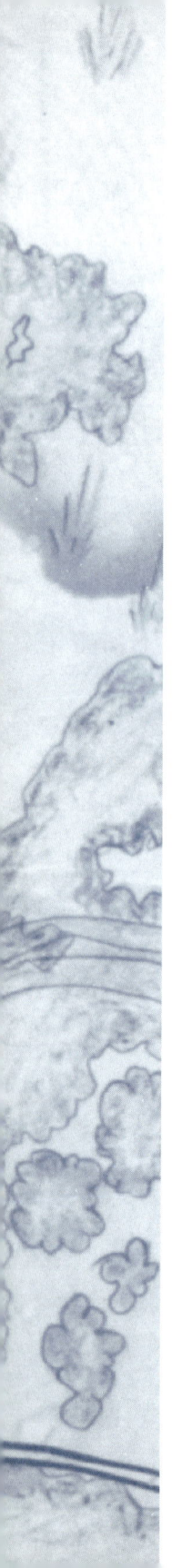

Contributors

Patti A. Abbott
Carolyn Anderson
Jodi A. Bakkum
Pamela Barge, D.C.
Linda Benjamin
Lydia Brewster
Mary Jane Brindley
Kris Brose
Rick Brown
Elizabeth Brudus
Maretta Joy Budde
Claire Burkard
Jean Ann Burkard
Camp Ehawee
Mark Cassellius, D.C.
Gail K. Cleary
Kristine Cleary
Sandra Cleary
Megan Coffey
Sara Coffey
William Russell Coffey
Stephanie A. Cooper
Virginia Dale
Laurie Davis
Ruth Nixon Davy
Jeanne Dawson
Diet Center
Beverly DiNicola
Erika Dreger
Jane Ebersberger
Barbara Fisher
Susan Fukuda
Alice Engelhard Gassere

Ruth Gautsch
Nancy Geiger
Mrs. Harry (Mary Ellen) Gouff
Gundersen Lutheran
   Medical Center
   Nutritional Services
Becky Halvorsen
Cathy Halvorsen
Miranda Handfelt
Helen Harold
Nicole L. Harris
Mike Hayes
Judy Healy
Katherine Heise
Russell Philip Heise
Martha Hoffland
Mildred B. Hoover
Megan Hovre
Catherine Jambois
Kaitlin Janzen
Suzan Janzen
Joan Johnson
Sharon Jolivette
Elizabeth Kroker
La Crosse County
   Historical Society
LaVon Ladsten
Jackie Lamb
Leslie and Harley Large
Barb Larsen
Little Brownie Bakers
Donna Loveland
Linette Maloney

Melody Maloney
Amber Maly
Mary Mara
Amanda Marco
Arden (Bunny) Markos
Marshall Fields
Judy McHugh
Naomi Meinertz
Kathy Michelson
Lori Moe
Angie Moen
Jan Moore
McKenzie Mullen-Burkhart
Michelle Mullen-Burkhart
Muriel C. Mullen-Burkhart
Kathy Noel
Ocean Spray
Courtney Oldenburg
Sally Olson
Mary Lee Pedretti
Mary Pronschinske
Meagan Pronschinske
Sarah Resch
Faye Moseley Rezin
Lorraine Riedl
Katie Robertson
Mary Rohrer
Jane Ronnfeldt
Emily Root
Janet Roth
Ginny Schroeder
Alysha Scott-Muller
Beth Seebach

Rachel Seebach
Savannah Shortess
Nicole Skarda
Colleen Skinner
Jill Smick
Camille Smith
Emile Smith
Robert Smith
Sally K. Snow
Brooke Staskal
Donna Stebbins
Britt Stromquist
Amy Sullivan
Beverly Sura
Carol Taebel
Dawn Tuchner
Jenna Vogel
Marcia Wantock
Gloria Weisbecker
Alexandra Wiederholt
JoAnn Wiederholt
Gina Wilkins
Georgina Wilkins
Peter Wilkins
Sydney Wilkins
Sally Cremer Williams
Katie Wilson
Winding Rivers Library–LaCrosse, WI
Nancy Wohlert
Wolter Chiropractic Center
Diane Wood
Kay Wright
Bonnie L. Young

Index

Appetizers. *See also* Dips; Pizza; Snacks; Spreads
Broccoli Ham Ring, 56
Chicken Tortilla Roll-ups, 57
Grilled Vegetable Pizza Appetizers, 29
Ham Pickle Spears, 58
Mango Salsa, 73
Salmon Cocktail Balls, 60

Apple
Alabama Pudding, 49
Apple Raisin Wild Rice Pilaf, 84
Apple Soda, 64
Applesauce Cake, 144
Campfire Cobbler, 48
Caramel Apple Dip, 52
Favorite Apple Crisp, 138
Girl Scout Crunchy Caramel Apples, 136

Banana
Banana Boats, 47
Banana Fruit Kabobs, 61
Banana Split Dessert, 138
Beat-the-Heat Smoothie, 66
Blueberry Smoothie, 67
Yogurt Sundae, 63

Beef. *See also* Ground Beef
After-Church Venison Stew, 102
Grilled Sauerbraten Steak, 33

Beverages
Apple Soda, 64
Beat-the-Heat Smoothie, 66
Blueberry Smoothie, 67
Frozen Fruit Slush, 65
Fruit Fizz, 64
Lemonade, 65
Peach Melba Smoothie, 67

Blueberry
Beat-the-Heat Smoothie, 66
Blueberry Smoothie, 67
Double-Good Blueberry Pie, 149
Fruit with Lime, 140

Breads
Garlic Breadsticks, 54
Swannie's Orange Honey Muffins, 54

Broccoli
Broccoli Ham Ring, 56
Broccoli Salad, 71
Raisin Broccoli Salad, 72

Cakes
Applesauce Cake, 144
Cherry Chocolate Cake, 146
Girl Scout Strawberry Angel Surprise, 148
Ice Cream Cone Cakes, 147
The Best Chocolate Cake, 145

Chicken
Chicken in the Woods, 38
Chicken Julienne, 116
Chicken Tenderloins with Cranberry Mustard Sauce, 90
Chicken Tortilla Roll-ups, 57
Chinatown Almond Chicken, 114
Country Chicken Chowder, 110
Cranberried Chicken, 91
Creamy Chicken and Rice, 117
Fabulous Chicken Salad, 75
Favorite Chicken Salad, 112
Field's Famous Chicken Potpie, 88
Honey Mustard Chicken, 115
Oriental Chicken Salad, 76
Speedy Paella, 118
Wisconsin Chicken Vegetable Soup, 107

Chocolate
Banana Boats, 47
Caramel Bars, 132
Cherry Chocolate Cake, 146
Chocolate Frosting, 146
Davy Crockett Bars, 133
Girl Scout Café au Mint Chocolate Pie, 150
Girl Scout Levitating Layers, 141
Girl Scout Mint Delight, 142
Girl Scout Super Samoa Surprise, 152
Haystackers, 47

Kit Kat Bars, 134
Oreo Cheesecake, 143
Shaggy Dogs, 48
Special K Bars, 136
The Best Chocolate Cake, 145

Cookies
Caramel Bars, 132
Cranberry Cookies, 129
Cranberry Cookies with Orange
    Glaze, 130
Davy Crockett Bars, 133
Kit Kat Bars, 134
Lace Cookies in a Jar, 131
Original Home-Baked Girl Scout
    Cookies, 128
Rhubarb Dream Bars, 135
Special K Bars, 136

Cranberry
Chicken Tenderloins with Cranberry
    Mustard Sauce, 90
Cranberried Chicken, 91
Cranberry Cookies, 129
Cranberry Cookies with Orange
    Glaze, 130
Cranberry-Stuffed Pork Chops, 93
Spicy Cranberry Pork Stir-Fry, 122

Desserts. *See also* Cakes; Cookies; Pies
Alabama Pudding, 49
Angels on Horseback, 46
Banana Boats, 47
Banana Split Dessert, 138
Campfire Cobbler, 48
Favorite Apple Crisp, 138
Fruit with Lime, 140
Girl Scout Crunchy Caramel
    Apples, 136
Girl Scout Levitating Layers, 141
Girl Scout Mint Delight, 142
Haystackers, 47
Old-Fashioned Vanilla Ice
    Cream, 137
Oreo Cheesecake, 143
Shaggy Dogs, 48
Yogurt Sundae, 63

Dips
Caramel Apple Dip, 52
Pretzel Dip, 52
Seven-Layer Southwestern Dip, 53
Spicy Vegetable Dip, 53

Duck
Grilled River Duck Breasts, 91
Sweet River Duck, 92

Egg Dishes
Outdoor Omelets, 32

Fish
Crispy Catfish, 94
Grilled Marinated Walleye, 41
Lemon and Herb Grilled Trout, 40
Limey Muskie (Muskellunge), 96
Salmon Cocktail Balls, 60
Smoked Salmon Spread, 59
Spicy Catfish, 95
Stuffed Brook Trout, 97

Fruit. *See also* Apple; Banana; Blueberry;
    Cranberry; Grape; Salads, Fruits;
    Strawberry
Frozen Fruit Slush, 65
Fruit with Lime, 140
Mango Salsa, 73
Peach Melba Smoothie, 67
Rhurbarb Dream Bars, 135

Game. *See* Duck; Venison

Glazes and Frostings
Chocolate Frosting, 146
Orange Glaze, 130

Grape
Banana Fruit Kabobs, 61
Fabulous Chicken Salad, 75
Favorite Chicken Salad, 112
Grape Salad, 74

Grains. *See also* Rice
Couscous, 37
Two-Grain Vegetable Casserole, 82

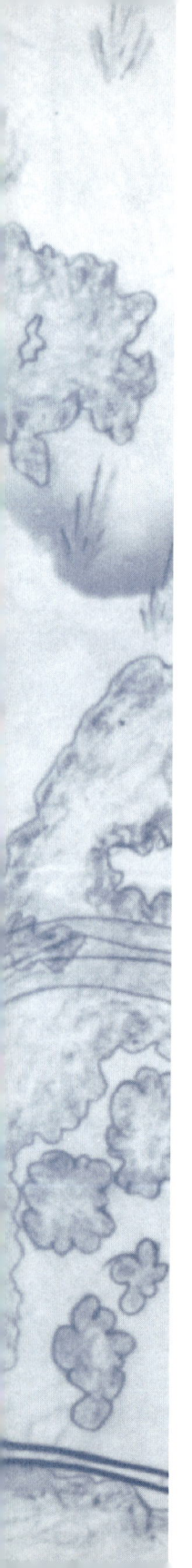

Ground Beef
    Beef and Bean Burritos, 119
    Curly Noodle Ground Beef
        Dinner, 120
    Enchilada Pie, 34
    Mock Enchiladas, 35
    Pioneer Beans, 43
    Sloppy Joes, 120
    Taco Pie, 121
    Taco Salad, 77

Ground Turkey
    Curly Noodle Ground Turkey
        Dinner, 120
    Mock Enchiladas, 35

Ham
    Broccoli Ham Ring, 56
    Ham Pickle Spears, 58

Lamb
    Lamb Kabobs with Couscous, 37

Marinade
    Seafood Marinade, 41

Outdoor Cooking
    Alabama Pudding, 49
    Angels on Horseback, 46
    Banana Boats, 47
    Barbecued Shrimp, 42
    Campfire Cobbler, 48
    Campfire Potatoes, 44
    Chicken in the Woods, 38
    Enchilada Pie, 34
    Girl Scout Cookout Checklist, 28
    Grilled Marinated Walleye, 41
    Grilled Pork Tenderloin, 36
    Grilled River Duck Breasts, 91
    Grilled Sauerbraten Steak, 33
    Grilled Smoked Turkey
        Quesadillas, 39
    Grilled Tomato Salad Pizza, 30
    Grilled Vegetable Pizza Appetizers, 29
    Haystackers, 47
    Lamb Kabobs with Couscous, 37
    Lemon and Herb Grilled Trout, 40
    Mock Enchiladas, 35
    Outdoor Omelets, 32
    Outdoor Vegetables, 45
    Pioneer Beans, 43
    Pizza Pudgy Pies, 31
    Practical Outdoor Cooking, 26
    Shaggy Dogs, 48
    Stuffed Brook Trout, 97
    Venison Steaks, 98

Pasta
    Artichoke Pesto Pasta, 125

Pies
    Double-Good Blueberry Pie, 149
    Girl Scout Café au Mint Chocolate
        Pie, 150
    Girl Scout Southern Peanut Butter
        Pie, 150
    Girl Scout Super Samoa Surprise, 152
    Strawberry Glaze Pie, 153

Pizza
    Grilled Tomato Salad Pizza, 30
    Grilled Vegetable Pizza Appetizers, 29
    Lunch Box Pizzas, 111
    Miniature Pita Pizza, 58
    Pizza Pudgy Pies, 31

Pork. *See also* Ham; Sausage
    Cranberry-Stuffed Pork Chops, 93
    Grilled Pork Tenderloin, 36
    Outdoor Omelets, 32
    Spicy Cranberry Pork Stir-Fry, 122

Potato
    Campfire Potatoes, 44
    Outdoor Vegetables, 45
    Potatoes Elegante, 80

Poultry. *See* Chicken; Turkey

Rice
    Apple Raisin Wild Rice Pilaf, 84
    Brown Rice Salad with Mango Salsa, 73
    Creamy Chicken and Rice Soup, 117
    Pumpkin Wild Rice Soup, 104

Speedy Paella, 118
Spiced Rice with Almonds, 85
Wild Rice Chick-Pea Shrimp Salad, 78

Rubs
Southern-Style Barbecue Rub, 40

Salad Dressings
Dressing for Girl Scout Greens, 70
Lemon Vinaigrette, 78
Raspberry Poppy Seed Vinaigrette, 70

Salads
Bok Choy Salad, 71
Broccoli Salad, 71
Brown Rice Salad with Mango Salsa, 73
Fabulous Chicken Salad, 75
Favorite Chicken Salad, 112
Oriental Chicken Salad, 76
Raisin Broccoli Salad, 72
Seafood Salad, 113
Spinach and Roasted Garlic Salad, 72
Taco Salad, 77
Wild Rice Chick-Pea Shrimp Salad, 78

Salads, Fruit
Banana Fruit Kabobs, 61
Fruit Salad, 61
Grape Salad, 74

Sausage
Honey Mustard Kabobs, 124
Pizza Pudgy Pies, 31
Sausage Bail-Out, 123

Seafood. *See also* Fish; Shrimp
Seafood Salad, 113

Shrimp
Barbecued Shrimp, 42
Speedy Paella, 118
Wild Rice Chick-Pea Shrimp Salad, 78

Side Dishes. *See also* Rice
Morels in Puff Pastry, 103
Mushroom Strudel, 83

Snacks
Honey-Glazed Snack Mix, 62
Jack-O'-Lantern Jumble, 62
Oyster Cracker Snack, 63

Soups and Stew
After-Church Venison Stew, 102
Country Chicken Chowder, 110
German Vegetable Soup, 106
Pumpkin Wild Rice Soup, 104
Wisconsin Chicken Vegetable Soup, 107

Spreads
Smoked Salmon Spread, 59

Strawberry
Banana Fruit Kabobs, 61
Beat-the-Heat Smoothie, 66
Fruit with Lime, 140
Girl Scout Strawberry Angel Surprise, 148
Strawberry Glaze Pie, 153

Turkey. *See also* Ground Turkey
Grilled Smoked Turkey Quesadillas, 39

Vegetables. *See also* Broccoli; Potato
Artichoke Pesto Pasta, 125
German Vegetable Soup, 106
Glazed Carrots with Dill, 79
Outdoor Vegetables, 45
Pineapple-Glazed Yams, 81
Pioneer Beans, 43
Pumpkin Wild Rice Soup, 104
Two-Grain Vegetable Casserole, 82
Wilted Dandelions, 104
Wisconsin Chicken Vegetable Soup, 107

Venison
After-Church Venison Stew, 102
Settler's Venison, 98
Venison Fingers, 100
Venison Steaks, 98
Venison Stroganoff, 101

Hope's Bounty
Recipes and Remembrances

Girl Scouts of Riverland Council
2710 Quarry Road
La Crosse, Wisconsin 54601
800-78-SCOUT (800-787-2688)
email: girlscouts@centuryinter.net
www.gsriverland.com

Please send _____ copies of *Hope's Bounty* at $16.95 each $ _____

Wisconsin residents add sales tax at $0.93 each $ _____

Add postage and handling at $2.00 each $ _____

Total $ _____

_____
Name

_____
Street Address

_____
City   State   Zip

_____
Telephone

Method of Payment: [ ] MasterCard   [ ] VISA
                       [ ] Check payable to Girl Scouts of Riverland Council

_____
Account Number   Expiration Date

_____
Signature

Photocopies will be accepted.